Transport and Distribution in the Single Market

Transport and Distribution in the Single Market

TNT Express

With a Foreword by
Karel Van Miert,
EC Commissioner responsible for transport

Published in association with CBI Initiative 1992

First published in 1990 by Mercury Books
Published in paperback 1992
by Mercury Books
Gold Arrow Publications Ltd
862 Garratt Lane, London SW17 0NB

Set in Plantin by Phoenix Photosetting, Chatham
Printed and bound in Great Britain by
Mackays of Chatham PLC, Chatham, Kent

British Library Cataloguing in Publication Data

Transport and distribution.
1. European Community Countries. Distribution trades
I. TNT Express II. CBI Initiative 1992

ISBN 1-85252-101-5

The Confederation of British Industry (CBI) is actively engaged in a wide range of EC policy issues through its offices in London and Brussels, and each quarter it issues a briefing pack, *Europe sans Frontieres*, on EC legislative developments. In 1988 the CBI launched a campaign, Initiative 1992, to equip British companies with practical advice and information on operating in the single market. This book forms part of that campaign.

Contents

Foreword

In a fast-changing Europe, where expanding business goes along with new opportunities, no progress could be achieved without improved mobility of people and goods. That is why Common Transport Policy plays such an important role in the achievement of the single market.

Although transport was one of the European common policies explicitly mentioned in the Treaty of Rome, progress could not be achieved as successfully as in other economic fields until the mid-eighties, when the dynamics of the single market programme, among others, brought pressure to bear.

What are the main objectives of transport policy? I would say, above all, to serve consumers and businesses properly, meeting their real needs and anticipating new ones. Also to serve society as a whole by drafting into European transport legislation important general factors such as safety, environment and framing the social role of transport.

Economic operators know what we are talking about: in the last five years, the freedom to provide transport services has been progressively introduced within the Community, allowing more competition, new opportunities and better (and sometimes cheaper) services to users. This liberalisation process is accompanied by harmonisation measures, in such areas as taxation, working conditions and professional standards for transport operators. At the same time, the application of competition rules is being reinforced, notwithstanding the concession of group exemptions: agreements between undertakings can bring improvements to the organisation of the transport services and to consumers. Examination of state aids as well as exclusive rights held by certain transport companies are now becoming major preoccupations of the Community. Last, but not least, the Community is taking action to define and assist in the setting up of pan-European integrated transport networks and transport infrastructure.

The development and improvement of transport services needs, however, to be put in line with such requirements as environment protection, higher safety standards and the tackling of traffic congestion. The external costs of transport must be reduced in order to develop a pattern of 'sustainable mobility'.

Finally, as vital transport activities extend beyond the Community's external frontiers, external relations in the transport field are becoming increasingly important. The Community as a whole is now called upon to adopt a common position vis-à-vis countries outside the EC.

The common transport policy is in a state of radical change. From now on transport operators will have to forgo a situation where national barriers allow protected markets. We are moving in the direction of a larger, more efficient market, where the opportunities for business are greater, but so also is competition. The economy, and consumers in particular, will be the beneficiaries of this new, more efficient transport system.

Karel Van Miert,
EC Commissioner responsible for transport

Preface

CBI Initiative 1992 has a vital role to play in informing British industry about the opportunities which will occur as the single European market is created, and TNT Express is pleased to be the Founder Member for transport and distribution.

In writing this book, TNT Express aims to help executives evaluate their own situation in the light of the new conditions and to suggest ways in which distribution can be used as a weapon to gain competitive edge.

The book draws out the significant changes which are likely to take place in the transport industry up to and beyond 1992. We have examined the impact of the proposed legislation on each transport mode and offer practical advice on how to develop a distribution strategy which will meet the new challenges of a Europe without frontiers. The book concludes with a guide to each transport market in the EC.

TNT Express is a pan-European oganisation and the experience we have gained through servicing client companies from every sector of industry and commerce in the UK and across the Continent is reflected in this book.

As the single market develops and trade between the member states increases so the importance of transport and distribution will grow. Our industry will not only help the free flow of goods from one member state to another but will also become a cutting edge for companies to improve their customer service levels and efficiency. New pan-European transport systems have already emerged and will further develop to help industry and commerce seize the exciting trade opportunities which 1992 will bring.

The approach we have taken towards our European business has been straightforward – to concentrate on the things that we do best. TNT Express has developed an advanced and reliable express transport system which allows users to develop their European businesses. This has led us to build businesses locally within each individual member state and also to create a European system for European companies. We are happy to pass on the knowledge we have gained during this process as part of our contribution to CBI Initiative 1992.

We have written this book in the hope that readers will find it a useful guide to the opportunities of 1992 and the opportunities that transport and distribution has to offer.

Sir Peter Abeles
Chief Executive
TNT Limited

Introduction

The objective of the single European market is to create an EC market with no barriers to trade. This new enlarged market of some 320 million consumers will give European industry an opportunity to improve its competitiveness by reducing costs and by encouraging commercial, technical and research and development co-operation. In theory, if all the measures outlined in the Single European Act are introduced, unemployment will be reduced, growth rates will increase and a better balance in the world economy will develop.*

In his report 'The cost of non-Europe', Paolo Cecchini said he believed that the completion of the single market will have the effect of giving consumers a substantial gain, as prices drop and product quality and choice increase under the impact of open competition. For manufacturers, though, he believed that the outlook was more mixed. Under the pressure of new competition, it is likely that profit margins are going to be squeezed, especially in those companies with some sort of monopoly or protected position. The successful companies will be those that respond to the new competitive environment by scaling up production, gaining experience and eliminating management inefficiencies.

Companies will have the opportunity to develop greater economies of scale from existing manufacturing plants by expanding their markets throughout the EC. However, in order to do this, one vital factor will be the provision of a European distribution system which will allow companies to match or exceed existing service levels and service overseas clients on the same basis as domestic clients. There are, however, dangers to this strategy.

Firstly, European competitors will look towards the UK home market in order to gain their own economies of scale. This could result in a reduction in home market share for UK companies, pressure on domestic prices and the loss of some economies of scale.

Secondly, if the distribution system selected or strategy followed is not sufficient to its task, costs could escalate and there would be a

* This book was compiled with information current, in general, at July 1989 and subsquently updated in July 1991 to include the latest EC-related developments.

failure to meet local suppliers' service criteria. This could result from the use of the wrong carrier, the use of the wrong distribution system or a lack of control or innovation in the distribution function.

The transport system services all the manufacturing and retailing industries, which are going to have to adapt and change to meet the needs of the single market. For this reason it is important to have an efficient transport industry which is capable of meeting these changing needs.

The objective of the Commission's 1992 programme is envisaged by the Community's 1985 White Paper 'Completing the internal market', which includes two types of proposals that will have an impact on the movement of goods within Europe. Firstly, there are proposals which are specifically adopted to make transport easier and subject to less regulation. Secondly, there are proposals with a broader general objective, which will have an impact on the whole business sector.

The 1992 programme does not attempt to influence directly the methods of transport of goods within member states but rather to provide a liberalised and harmonised environment for transport companies to operate in. This new environment will of course not only be to the benefit of transport companies but will allow a whole range of companies to examine their distribution strategies and put in place more efficient systems.

The impact of 1992 on transport users will depend on the extent to which industry embraces the concept of a European distribution strategy. The rationalisation of legislation and the deregulation of the transport industry will give users the opportunity to plan their distribution on a European scale. Companies that embrace this concept will be able to take advantage of improved customer service levels and possibly reduce total distribution costs. However, any company expecting a bonanza of cheap transport after 1992 may well be disappointed.

As 1992 approaches, the need to have a European distribution strategy is a real one. A properly thought-out distribution strategy will provide a better level of service and improve a company's efficiency and competitiveness. The objectives, however, of this strategy need to be accurately defined in terms of understanding, anticipating and satisfying customers' requirements.

The development of a distribution strategy is usually a gradual process which examines what is currently being provided and determines areas of improvement. This by necessity needs to be a step-by-step process and involves nearly all the functions of the company, from sales to manufacturing. At this stage it will be necessary for the company to make a strategic decision either to contract out its distribution or handle the whole process in-house. The current trend is for more and more companies to elect to contract out, either through third-party network services or through dedicated distribution services. Selection of the correct service will of course be an important element in the distribution strategy.

To be successful in the single market companies will need to have an efficient distribution system which consistently delivers the required level of service to satisfy their European customers.

I

The legislative programme

1. The removal of physical barriers to trade

The concept of the single market calls for the free movement of goods between the member states. This would mean that customs formalities should be removed for goods transported within the EC. To achieve this it will be necessary either to remove or to reform the huge amount of work carried out at international borders.

Currently, customs authorities at each border carry out a number of different checks in relation to the movement of goods. These include inspection of goods, checking of customs paperwork, collection of VAT on imports, anti-smuggling procedures, checking of vehicle safety standards, checking of hauliers' licences, collection of trade statistics, checking of animal and plant health and calculation of monetary compensatory amount for agricultural produce.

The majority of these checks could be carried out anywhere, but historically the borders have become convenient points. Therefore, a whole industry has grown up around customs checks, which has had the effect of slowing down the movement of goods and adding considerable administrative costs to hauliers and transport users.

Proposed reforms to the whole area of customs procedures have not yet been finalised, but the proposals laid out are wide-ranging and radical. The objectives of the proposals will be to speed up the movement of goods across borders, allowing carriers and transport users to schedule vehicles and predict transit times accurately. The effect of this faster movement will be to create a more efficient transport industry. In this chapter the following topics will be examined in the light of the Commission's proposals:

- VAT collection
- Excise duty
- Customs procedures and physical checks
- EFTA
- Third countries

- Inland clearance depots and the fast lane
- Animal and plant health borders
- The collection of trade statistics
- Monetary compensatory amounts

VAT collection

The single market programme envisages free movement of goods between all member states of the EC without hindrance from fiscal distortions or other obstacles. At present a common VAT system applies in principle throughout the EC, although rates charged vary considerably. For example, the UK uses zero-rating for a range of goods and services and a standard rate of 17.5 per cent for everything else. Other countries, for example Italy, apply a lower, standard and upper rate of VAT.

Under current VAT regulations all exports are zero-rated and VAT is payable on all imports at the point of entry into the country at the local importing country's rate. To pay the VAT there are two systems:

- An importer or a transport company sets up a deferment account, backed by a bank guarantee with the customs authorities. All VAT monies due are debited against this account, which is topped up on a regular basis.
- Alternatively, an importer can pay any VAT monies due by a banker's draft or cash before the goods are released from customs.

Over the last year or so the European Commission has accepted the need for greater flexibility in the medium term, but without sacrificing the goal of eventual harmonisation which, in its original proposals, envisaged two basic charge bands, one of 4–9 per cent and the other of 14–20 per cent, with no zero-rating.

The Commission also remains committed to its original idea that VAT should be charged on goods before export, i.e. in the country of origin, and recovered in the country of desination. For example, a UK supplier selling to a trader in France would charge 17.5 per cent to his customer who would then, assuming the latter was registered in France for VAT purposes, reclaim the tax from the French authorities. Such a system would require some form of clearing house to adjust the balances between the member states. Because this was not politically acceptable to the majority of member states, the Commission was instructed to introduce a transitional regime based on the destination principle which will work as follows:

- Exports would continue to be zero-rated and VAT would be paid by the importer at the local importing country rate.
- Registered businesses would account for VAT on supplies from other EC countries as part of their normal domestic VAT system, eliminating the need for border delays.
- A more sophisticated electronic data interchange (EDI) system would be introduced to help monitor the paperwork.

From a transport point of view both proposed systems would simplify the current VAT collection system. Under the clearing-house principle, it would be the responsibility of the exporters and importers to collect and pay the VAT. The transporter would no longer be involved.

The physical collection of VAT monies due under the destination principle would be relatively simple. Importers would no longer need to have their own deferment account against which all VAT due was debited. This would simplify procedures not only for customs authorities but also for hauliers and transport companies.

Excise duty

It is proposed to harmonise excise duties throughout the EC. The effect on tobacco, alcohol and petroleum products sold in the UK will be fairly dramatic, according to Price Waterhouse in their book in this series, *Tax: Strategic Corporate Tax Planning*. They suggest that the price of twenty cigarettes could be reduced by 40 pence, while a pint of beer may cost 20 pence more. The price of fuel would be relatively stable. Because of these price alterations health lobbies are opposing the changes and it seems likely that they may not be politically acceptable either.

A new system for dealing with excise goods – and specifically the movement of dutiable goods between member states – will be needed to allow for the planned disappearance of fiscal frontiers at the end of 1992.

Latest Commission thinking in that context involves substituting a system called REDS (Registered Excise Dealers and Shippers) for the existing network of EC bonded warehouses. This is intended to preserve the present arrangements under which goods can be transported between bonded warehouses without attracting any excise duties. Such duties only become liable for payment once goods leave the bonded facilities en route to customers.

However, it should be pointed out that at the time of writing, discussions on the whole subject of excise duty are still at a fairly early stage and ideas could change before the end of 1992.

Customs procedures and physical checks

At the heart of the development of the single market will be the effective dismantling of borders as far as the intra-EC movement of goods is concerned. Latest Commission thinking envisages replacing the border check system with roving customs officers who would have the authority to stop and spot-check vehicles and/or their contents within 50 kilometres of the point of entry into a country. Still to be resolved are questions such as where the spot checks will actually take place and how they will be organised. In addition, certain custom authorities, such as that of the UK, are concerned that the system will be open to abuse, especially by drugs smugglers and terrorists. It remains to be seen whether that concern will lead to the retention of some form of border checks.

Currently, intra-EC freight movements are based on the use of the Single Administrative Document (SAD) introduced in 1988 and the Community Transit (T-Form) system. Plans are for the SAD to be abolished for most intra-Community movements at the beginning of 1993, although it may well be retained for certain categories of Spanish and Portuguese traffic until they complete their EC accession period in 1995.

Use of the T-Form is also expected to be substantially reduced. The trader is currently required to demonstrate that the goods are in free circulation within the EC. Under the new arrangements the goods will be assumed to fall into that category unless there is documentation to show otherwise.

At the same time as the Commission proposes to abolish the physical borders, the paperwork could be handled by one form of the direct trader input (DTI) system. What seems certain is that by 1992 most importers and exporters should be on DTI, where the SAD is input to customs via one of the appropriate systems. These systems speed up the clearance of goods and enhance the controls applied by customs, some of which may be carried out before a cargo arrives at the port. Customs also set national and local parameters for goods to be examined – for instance, all cargo from a certain port or all cargo to a certain destination.

A further interesting principle that the Commission is trying to establish is the setting-up of rules which will force customs authorities to provide information. These rules will be binding not only on the individual member states' customs authorites who provide the information but on all Community customs authorities, regardless of which authority provided the information. The Commission believes this will help provide a uniform customs approach throughout the EC and secure a uniform application of Community customs law.

The Commission has decided that to take this approach for all customs-related matters would be too great a burden and has, therefore, decided to limit the scope of the rules to the classification of goods in customs nomenclature. However, this may give some indication to future thinking on customs-related matters and should help reduce uncertainty for traders.

EFTA

A meeting of the European Free Trade Association (EFTA) in February 1989 confirmed that all six members seek at least closer links with the EC. Each has agreed to the SAD for imports and exports and they look likely to harmonise increasingly with EC requirements in transport and other sectors.

Since EFTA countries have removed customs barriers to EC traffic and receive reciprocal freedom for their exports to the EC, common transport rules would be a desirable complement. However, at present Switzerland and Austria, for instance, have tax barriers to deter road transit traffic and Switzerland has a 28-tonne gross weight limit on trucks, although its vehicles are allowed to load to 40 tonnes before crossing the border into adjacent countries.

All six EFTA members are already environmentally aware and, as the environment becomes increasingly important in policy making within the EC, a comity of interest is likely. This may well lead to common rules on exhaust emissions, weights and noise.

In general, EFTA members stand to gain from reciprocal arrangements with the EC on transport matters, and not only in the field of road transport: Austria, for example, has a particular interest in the completion of the Rhine–Danube Canal.

Third countries

The principle on which the EC works is that goods imported from third countries, once they have been cleared through any member state's border, are deemed to be in free circulation. This means that these goods can be moved from one member state to another without further border delays or payment of any extra duties.

However, there are a few product sectors where national quotas have been allowed. For example, steel and textiles are subject to international agreements limiting volumes of imports. In addition, in some instances voluntary restraint agreements have been set up: an example of this is the negotiated limit on the sales of Japanese cars in the UK.

The Commission hopes eventually to remove national quotas either totally or, where justified, by changing a national quota into a Community quota. So, in future, affected goods will be cleared against an overall Community quota regardless of which individual member state they are imported to.

The Community is still fully committed to its existing international obligations such as those under the General Agreement on Tariffs and Trade (GATT) and the Organisation for Economic Co-operation and Development (OECD). The development of the EC's external policy will be in line with these agreements and the Community will not seek to protect its markets from goods imported from third countries.

The Community subscribes to the principle that international trade negotiations relating to goods should take place on the basis of a broad reciprocity of benefits: the idea is that by negotiating on a world scale and making 'trading concessions' every country wins. Services are not currently covered by GATT, but major negotiations are in progress in the GATT Uruguay round to extend GATT disciplines to services. The Community's external regime for services trade will be developed in this context, and the Community will resort to bilateral agreements with other countries only to remedy existing discrimination against EC interests and to contribute to wider liberalisation.

Local content and the origin of goods are two further factors which relate to the impact of the single market on third countries. Local content is allied to the question of inward investment by third countries, although neither the EC as a whole nor the UK have specific local content rules.

Origin of goods is basically a system whereby customs determine whether specific goods are subject to any special regime (preferential treatment for imports from specific countries, for example) or not. The single market programme will not affect the determination of the origin of goods, except where special regimes apply and in other limited cases. However, no other goods sold legally in the Community will have to meet origin or local content rules.

Where anti-dumping duties are already in force in the Community, in respect of specific items imported from third countries a special rule exists to permit the same duties to be levied on identical items assembled in the Community by the same interests, provided that *inter alia* over 60 per cent of the parts come from the country against which dumping was found.

The approach which the Commission will adopt on economic and commercial policy towards third countries was summed up in the statement following the Hanover European Council meeting in 1988. It noted that the internal market should not close in on itself. In conformity with the provisions of GATT, the Community should be open to third countries and must negotiate with those countries, where necessary, to ensure access to their markets for Community exports. It will seek to preserve the balance of advantages accorded, while respecting the unity and identity of the internal market of the Community.

Thus third countries as well as member states stand to benefit from the single market: there will be only one frontier to cross; product standards and certification will be uniform or at least universally recognised, and economies of scale will be possible owing to the size of the market.

Inland clearance depots and the fast lane

Inland clearance depots (ICDs) operate as customs clearance points but away from the major port areas. To use an ICD, goods are moved under seal through port areas with minimum delay, and customs clearance of the goods takes place at the ICD.

The ICD has become a major industry in itself with the growth of international air and road freight services and the transport to inland destinations of marine containers. For example, Northampton ICD is Britain's third largest port by number of customs entries.

Imported goods arrive at ICDs with export seals from the country of origin. The seals are checked at the ICD by customs, who have the option to perform full physical checks. At Northampton, much of the clearance work is done after customs have broken the seals.

The first step towards rapid clearance procedures have been made in the UK with the introduction of the fast-lane concept. The primary aim of the fast lane is to work within existing import controls but to reduce delays caused by customs clearance to the absolute minimum for goods imported from other member states. The fast-lane schemes are targeted at goods which are in free circulation within the EC for which customs interest is limited to the collection of statistical information, the collection of VAT and the discharging of any Community transit responsibilities.

Fast lane exploits the advantages of the current electronic system for processing import declarations or entries. Following an electronic entry, shipments eligible for fast-lane use are granted immediate clearance by the customs entry processing computer (DEPS – departmental entry processing system) provided any VAT due is secured by means of a computerised deferment account facility. Release of the shipment is then allowed, subject to any physical inspection of the goods. Presentation of the usual paper declaration and any supporting papers, including Community transit documents, are required within seventy-two hours of acceptance of the electronic entry by DEPS.

It is intended that there should be three fast-lane options which traders, agents or transport operators will be able to use:

- Direct trader input (DTI) is a facility which provides for the direct submission of electronic information to the customs computer. DTI involves the automatic identification by DEPS, following the normal electronic declaration, of shipments which can go fast lane and be immediately cleared provided VAT is secured.
- Fast-lane period entry is a facility for regular importers with sophisticated computer systems who are authorised to provide data required by customs in electronic form on a monthly basis. This system allows accelerated clearance in the same way as DTI.
- The simplified period entry scheme (SPES) will offer importers the advantages of a simplified version of period entry. SPES will allow traders to provide customs with an electronic schedule of import information. VAT and statistical information will be captured on the trader's system, validated and transmitted to customs. It is expected that SPES will be available in late 1990.

To use the last two of these systems will require prior application to the customs authorities. They are not designed for *ad hoc* shipments. Fast-lane DTI is available automatically without prior customs authorisation.

But what future would ICDs have after 1992? There would be no real benefit in an agent bringing freight into an ICD when he could do all necessary clearance at a port, and it may be used only to clear goods from outside the EC. The more far-sighted ICD operators have planned for this eventuality and are taking action now.

As the major non-EC trading countries would be the USA, Japan and EFTA, ICDs could find themselves working as distribution centres to send items produced in the USA, Japan and EFTA throughout the EC. It seems likely that ICD rules will be relaxed after

1992 to come into line with the less stringent requirements of local import control. For instance, whereas an ICD needs physical barriers between import and export goods, a local import control point needs only white lines between the two traffics.

Animal and plant health

A new set of borders could be created to cope with animal and health regulations. Some would be in line with existing national boundaries – for instance the border for checking animals for equine horse fever could equate with that of Spain, because Spain is so far the only country to be affected.

On the other hand, the boundary for rabies is somewhere in the middle of France, because the authorities believe northern France is clear of the disease. Customs work could therefore be swapped from one border to another.

The collection of trade statistics

The Commission has published its proposals for the collection of intra-Community trade statistics after the removal of the barriers. The system proposed would use existing administrative networks and broadly proposes using VAT returns. This would allow statistical information to be collected without increasing the number of indirect checks or increasing the burdens on tax payers.

Although the Commission proposes using existing sources to provide the information, it has also proposed that the main parties concerned with the provision of the information should be identified and used to help develop a modern data transmission system to take away the administrative burden. This system is to be called Intrasat.

Monetary compensatory amounts

Under the common agricultural policy, agricultural transactions are carried out at an artificial 'green' monetary exchange rate and compensation is paid to make up for the difference between that rate and the real one.

Current proposals are for such compensation to be suspended and for agricultural trade to be carried on at the real exchange rate.

There would be no refunds or repayments, which would at least save customs the work involved in calculating the amounts.

2. The liberalisation of the transport system

The liberalisation of transport throughout the EC will free the transport industry from the mass of national and EC legislation which has stifled competition and limited capacity.

This chapter examines how the legislation will be lifted and the likely impact of this on transport companies. The changes described will apply only to the hire and reward operators, who include hauliers and distribution contractors. Nothing in the EC plan suggests that cabotage or free operation will be extended to own-account operators.

The majority of liberalising measures affecting the transport system up to and after 1992 will be aimed at the road, inland water, shipping and air transportation sectors. The main reasons for this are that these sectors have traditionally been controlled by national regulations and they are the sectors where private operators dominate the provision of services.

Road transport

The road transport sector is a major area for change for two key reasons.

Firstly, road transport is the dominant mode of transport for moving goods within the Community. In 1986 road haulage accounted for more than 87 per cent of goods transported by weight across EC borders. Road haulage is, therefore, the predominant method of transport for the manufacturing and retailing industries, who have to adapt and change to meet the needs of the new business environment created by the single market.

Secondly, in order to provide a mechanism for the free movement of goods it is important to have an efficient road transport industry. In this respect it will be necessary to reform the regulations, imposed at national and international level, which are out of date and are seen to restrict the efficiency of the industry.

National regulations are imposed to determine the criteria for entry to the road haulage business and to regulate the operational aspects of the business, such as operating hours and environmental concerns. These regulations are determined by each individual country and result in a number of widely differing regimes.

For international transport each member state receives a limited number of permits under which its hauliers can perform international work. The number of permits is controlled by a series of bilateral agreements between the twelve member states. The actual number of permits between any two countries is agreed by representatives who meet on a regular basis. For UK hauliers permits are not required for intra-EC journeys between the UK and the Netherlands, Belgium, Luxembourg, Greece and Denmark. This system results in an imbalance of capacity in the industry which is further compounded by the imbalance in intra-Community trade.

The more liberal countries such as the Netherlands and the UK set the number of permits so high that they are never likely to represent a limitation on capacity. But other countries do restrict the number of permits available. This permit system also causes problems for cross-trading operators. For example a UK haulier who wishes to move goods between France and Italy may not get a permit. This results in inefficiencies such as empty running.

Domestic road transport

The UK used to operate a quantitative system of operator licensing but controls over the number of carriers operating in the domestic market were abolished in 1968. Since then the emphasis has been on quality control, and operator licensing provides the means of judging and controlling the overall performance of operators. Applicants for an 'O' licence need to satisfy a number of requirements such as good repute, financial standing, professional competence, satisfactory vehicle maintenance arrangements and, for goods vehicle operating centres, environmental suitability, before being granted a licence. Licences are issued for a fixed term of up to 5 years. A new licence must then be applied for.

The UK requirements of good repute, financial standing and professional competence are embodied in an EC directive on admission to the occupation of road haulage operator. That directive applies in all member states to operators in the hire or reward sector using vehicles over 6 tonnes gross weight. It distinguishes between domestic and international operators for the purposes of assessing financial standing and in terms of the qualifications needed to satisfy the professional competence requirement.

The Government is reviewing domestic 'O' licensing arrangements to examine the scope for reducing the licensing burden on industry, bearing in mind existing requirements under EC legislation.

International road transport

It is planned to remove the international bilateral agreement structure so that international road transport companies will be able to move goods between any member state. After 1992, member states will no longer be allowed to restrict the number of hauliers entering their international road transport markets.

The Council agreed in 1988 that, as from 1 January 1993, access to the EC international market for Community hauliers will be governed by a system of Community licences issued on the basis of qualitative criteria. The Council, acting on the basis of Commission proposals, is required to decide the necessary measures to implement this by 30 June 1991.

All permits for road haulage in the EC will be abolished by the end of December 1992. In the run-up to that development, the EC multilateral permit quotas have been increased by 40 per cent per annum in recent years.

The UK domestic market will not be affected by the regulation, but UK international hauliers should benefit from the opening up of parts of the EC market which have hitherto been restricted.

Cabotage

Under the Treaty of Rome, the EC Transport Council is also obliged to decide the conditions under which domestic road transport in one member state may be undertaken by a haulier registered in another member state. This practice, known as 'cabotage', was not allowed until recently in any member state.

However, over the last couple of years, EC states have begun to make some progress on that issue by allowing a limited number of cabotage journeys to take place. Currently, 15,000 permits are available to companies within the EC, each one allowing the operator to make cabotage journeys for a two-month period. Member states may choose to double the number of permits available to them by halving their period of validity to one month – the UK has adopted this option. Vehicles engaged in cabotage work are subject to many of the regulations of the state where the work is carried out, a situation which is at present causing considerable complications. For example, while the host country's laws apply to issues such as pricing, contracts, vehicle weights and dimensions, work and rest hours, etc., other matters including social security, vehicle registration and taxation come under the jurisdiction of the operator's home country.

Transit countries

Separate negotiations have been taking place between the EC, Switzerland, Austria and Yugoslavia on the question of transit of goods through their countries. In the case of Switzerland and Austria in particular, the issue has in fact caused serious political problems between those countries and the EC.

The EC wants to see the development of Alpine transit 'corridors' for trucks up to 40 tonnes. The Swiss and the Austrians, though, are opposed to any increase in international heavy goods vehicle traffic on their roads, primarily for environmental reasons. In that context, the Swiss, for example, have consistently refused to lift their established night-time ban on most truck movements, a ban originally imposed to cut down on noise nuisance. The Austrians also imposed a night-time ban on trucks. Both the Swiss and the Austrians insist there should be much greater use of rail/road combined transport, with freight being moved across the Alps by rail rather than by road. The EC accepts the principle of greater use of combined transport, but claims current railway capacity through Switzerland and Austria is insufficient to meet traffic demands.

At the time of writing, Swiss Transport Minister Adolf Ogi had just made what he described as a 'final offer' to the EC to try and resolve the Alpine transit dispute. The Swiss offer involves retention of an existing 28-tonne weight limit for trucks, with some exceptions for vehicles carrying perishable cargoes. The EC is thought unlikely to accept the offer and the whole subject is likely to become linked with general moves to develop a free trade agreement between the EC and the EFTA countries which include Switzerland and Austria.

Yugoslavia has generally been willing to accept transit traffic and has recently signed an agreement with the EC which, *inter alia*, provides EC funding for certain Yugoslavian infrastructure projects. This agreement is, however, currently on ice due to the political situation in Yugoslavia.

Shipping

Traditionally a third country's shipping lines have always been able to carry goods between any other countries, and that situation paved the way for the growth to worldwide dominance of the UK merchant shipping fleet in the last century. The dominance has declined with the growth of flags of convenience and other nations' national shipping fleets. EC policy so far has been aimed at trying to protect the merchant shipping fleets of all its member countries from 'unfair' competition.

Transport Commissioner Karel van Miert has been drawing up a shipping subsidy plan. His proposals include a series of measures linked to the formation of a single European flag (EUROS) to replace the separate national flags. This could affect ships operating under the Manx flag, which has been set up as a 'tax efficient' flag registry within the EC.

Gibraltar, currently an associate member of the EC, might also be affected. Under the van Miert plan, European sailors will become exempt from paying personal income tax, thereby reducing shipowners' overall crewing costs.

The plan also envisages making technical and safety certificates issued to ships by any EC nation acceptable throughout the Community, and grants from the EC's research and development fund could be made available to produce more efficient designs of ship.

Technically advanced ship designs, using fewer crew members and less fuel, would ultimately be more competitive. It remains to be seen whether the EC will go all the way and institute a scrap-and-build policy to replace older ships with new ones, but if this policy was adopted then obviously a financial gain would be made by the countries that have a modern and efficient shipbuilding industry.

If it did so, it seems likely that replacement ships built under the policy, and presumably with more EC grant aid, would have to be built in European shipyards. The EC's shipping proposals are designed to maintain as many European seafaring jobs as possible as well as trying to reduce the cost difference between operating ships under the European flag and under flags of convenience.

There is already a European shipbuilding subsidy, and if and when the van Miert plan comes to fruition any financial benefits available to European shipowners will run along the same lines. At present operators of bulk ships get more financial aid than do operators of container ships because bulk ships are more expensive to run.

Aid will be administered through the relevant government departments in the individual states. The EC has tended to take a different tack on matters relating to shipping from that which it takes on other transport modes.

Still to be published at the time of writing are details of a proposed block exemption from EC competition rules for liner shipping consortia. Shipping conferences already have a block exemption from the

Treaty of Rome's competition provisions subject to meeting certain regulations. For instance, they must not combine to eliminate competition and they must consult with users on issues such as rate increases.

Liner shipping consortia differ from conferences in that members normally work much more closely together. Conference members co-operate on general issues such as rates, but consortia often also work together on vessel pooling, general operations and even marketing. Major conferences may well, in fact, include one or more consortia.

The EC has now agreed that shipping consortia can now also be given block exemption from competition rules, but is still discussing the requirements which such groups will have to meet. The conditions are likely to differ considerably from those which currently apply to conferences.

Air cargo

A third package of European air transport liberalisation measures, due to have been presented by the European Commission this summer, should mark the final stage in the development of the EC's open skies policy. However, with a number of member states thought likely to have some reservations about various aspects of full liberalisation, the measures are not expected to gain formal approval until next year.

The latest EC package of measures was expected to include common criteria for airline and route licensing; the introduction of cabotage, enabling an airline from one country to offer domestic services in another; the complete phasing out of capacity restrictions; and the generalisation of fifth freedom rights allowing a carrier from one country to pick up traffic on intermediate routes within the EC.

EC transport ministers have, in fact, already agreed to end bilateral capacity and revenue-sharing agreements for scheduled airline operations within the EC. On the airfreight side, though, debate continues over the current EC stipulation that only companies which are licensed as EC cargo carriers will be able to make full use of the new liberalised traffic rights. As things stand at present, any non-EC national company providing air cargo services, but not holding an air transport licence, is excluded from being a Community air cargo carrier. Not surprisingly, that stipulation has provoked a strong response from some of the major non-European integrators active in Europe and they are continuing to lobby for the right to be classified as EC cargo carriers.

On a broader front, the European Commission is also keen to negotiate more liberalised air transport agreements with countries outside the Community, particularly the United States. It has been suggested in some quarters that such talks may well be linked with the issue of allowing certain non-European companies to gain designation eventually as EC cargo carriers.

On the environmental front, the EC is considering the phasing out of so-called 'chapter two' noisy aircraft in the Community, starting in 1995, over a seven- or eight-year period. That move could have particular implications for some parts of the airfreight and air express industry – it is reckoned that some 75 per cent of cargo aircraft are of the noisier 'chapter two' type rather than the quieter 'chapter three' category.

3. The harmonisation of transport regulations

The creation of the so-called 'level playing-field' for all companies in the EC has been a central theme of the Commission's thinking throughout its 1992 campaign. This 'level playing-field' in the transport market will be broadly achieved by the harmonisation of transport regulations in each member state. This should provide, in theory, equality of operators' costs throughout the Community.

Transport regulations have been different in each member state and the Commission has proposed a united approach to these regulations. The proposals would mean that companies would have to operate vehicles to the same standard in each member state. This applies not only to vehicle weights and dimensions, but to drivers' hours, safety equipment, road tax, fuel duty and member states' licensing systems.

Vehicle weights and dimensions

Harmonisation of vehicle weights and dimensions has now been agreed throughout the EC with the exception of maximum vehicle weights for the UK and the Republic of Ireland. Figure 1 shows the harmonised standards for vehicle weights and dimensions. However, it should be noted that these standards apply only to vehicles operating on international routes, and individual member states will be free to impose their own standards on vehicles used for domestic routes.

For domestic transport in the rest of the EC, other than the Republic of Ireland, both articulated and drawbar trucks can operate at 40 tonnes on five or six axles, with some countries allowing 44 tonnes and Belgium and the Netherlands going up to 50 tonnes.

The UK won its derogation on higher weight limits because the Department of Transport claimed that some 1,200 bridges would need to be strengthened in a 15-year programme to take the heavier weights.

The argument over allowing heavier vehicles on UK roads has been a high profile issue for many years now. Environmentalists say that the

Figure 1: Vehicle weight and dimension limits. European Commission proposals and existing UK regulations

	EC limit	UK limit
Maximum weight – articulated vehicles	40 tonnes	38 tonnes
Maximum weight – drawbar rigs	40 tonnes	32.52 tonnes
Maximum axle weight	11.5 tonnes	10.5 tonnes
Maximum length – articulated vehicles	16.5 metres	16.5 metres
Maximum length – drawbar rigs	18.35 metres	18 metres
Maximum width	2.5 metres	2.5 metres
Maximum width (refrigerated vehicles)	2.6 metres	2.6 metres
Maximum height	4 metres	No limit*

* except articulated vehicles over 32.5 tonnes, which have a height limit of 4.2 metres

heavier vehicles will do more damage to our roads and environment, while other experts argue that heavier trucks would not only reduce costs, but also mean fewer trucks on the roads. The UK Freight Transport Association, for example, not only wants the introduction of 40-tonne vehicles brought forward, but also supports a further increase in the size of vehicle allowed to include 44-tonners. Such a move, says the FTA, would reduce the number of vehicles on the roads by 9,000 and produce annual savings of 200 million litres diesel fuel.

However, while the UK government still looks determined to delay the advent of heavier trucks, it has sanctioned other changes in commercial vehicle legislation. In 1990, for example, it increased the overall length of articulated vehicles incorporating trailers from 15.5 metres to 16.5 metres, at the same time. This change followed amendment of the EC directive and whilst introducing controls on turning circles did, in effect, allow an increase in semi-trailer length and, therefore, volumetric carrying capacity. In connection with those changes, the UK Department of Transport sanctioned the use of a second kingpin on fifth wheel coupling equipment to allow greater use of existing tractor units at the new lengths.

Meanwhile, the EC has agreed a further directive, which came into force on 1 October 1991, covering the permitted lengths of roadtrains. Maximum permitted length of drawbar roadtrains will be 18.35 metres; maximum distance from front of loading area to rear of trailer will be 16 metres; and the maximum load dimension, i.e. the distance from the front of loading area to rear of trailer, minus the distance between the vehicle and trailer, 15.65 metres. Related changes in the UK's construction and use regulations are expected soon.

Vehicle excise and fuel duty

Vehicle excise and fuel duties are completely fragmented between each member state. Some nations, such as the French, operate low vehicle excise duty systems but impose road tolls, while UK operators pay fourteen times more vehicle excise duty than the Italians. However, the Department of Transport points out that the UK is the only member state fully to recover road infrastructure costs (costs of building, maintaining and policing the roads) through vehicle excise duty and fuel duty. All member states are being asked to adopt a similar system of infrastructure cost recovery through a Commission proposal on the charging of transport infrastructure costs to heavy goods vehicles.

To add to this confused situation, the German government caused a major row within the Community during 1990, when it attempted to introduce road tolls for commercial vehicles travelling through Germany. Industry observers felt the move was designed primarily to put pressure on the Commission to speed up plans for harmonising road transport operations – currently, the Germans believe their haulage industry is operating at a considerable disadvantage compared with competitors in other EC countries where road taxes and fuel costs are much lower. The German move was eventually stopped by a European Court injunction, but the general issue of road transport industry harmonisation is still far from being resolved.

Latest moves from the European Commission to achieve greater equality in the tax regimes for EC goods vehicles first involve establishing a common rate of fuel tax for derv. In 1991 ECOFIN agreed that, as from 1 January 1993, the minimum duty rate for derv shall be 245 Ecus per 1,000 litres. This compares with the current UK rate of 313 Ecus and a twelve nation average of 258 Ecus.

However, industry observers point out that even the introduction of common rates of fuel tax would not entirely resolve the problem of haulage industry inequalities among the dozen different member states. As a result, they say, fuel tax changes will need to go hand-in-hand with vehicle tax harmonisation moves.

The current differentials of vehicle tax are large and the Commission has therefore decided to propose minimum levels for 1992, 1993 and 1994 (see table on p. 28), with a view to further progress being made in 1995 once more data about costs has been collected from member states.

Categories of vehicles	Ecus			
	1992	1993	1994	Current UK
2 axled rigid 15–18 tonnes	645	860	1075	1759
4 axled rigid 29–31 tonnes	1267	1689	2111	3975
4 axled artic 31–33 tonnes	1097	1463	1829	3503
5 axled artic 36–38 tonnes	1216	1430	2027	4433

Source: Freight Transport Association

Another complication still to be resolved involves the question of tolls, which are imposed in some countries and not in others. The Commission has proposed that hauliers should be able to obtain a partial refund on their vehicle taxes on the basis of motorway tolls paid within the Community. It has been suggested that the method of reimbursement should be kept as simple as possible, but that hauliers seeking a refund would need to make a claim on the national authority of the member state in which the vehicle tax was paid.

The use of toll roads is more widespread on the Continent than in the UK and this proposal could mean a significant reduction in vehicle taxes collected by the UK government.

Drivers' hours

Current EC drivers' hours regulations focus on driving time, breaks, and daily, weekly and fortnightly rest periods. UK regulations, for example, state that drivers must take rest breaks totalling at least 45 minutes for each rolling period of 4.5 hours driving.

Now, though, the European Commission is proposing new legislation as part of its Social Charter which would include much wider provisions for all workers, including drivers. Proposals are likely to include a maximum 11-hour working day and a limit of eight hours for working at night.

UK transport industry operators are generally opposed to the proposals, claiming that the subject of drivers' hours is already adequately covered by existing regulations. They claim the proposed changes would unnecessarily complicate the planning of road transport journeys and push up overall transport costs.

Impact of harmonisation

Regardless of mode of transport, operators' costs are influenced by such factors as wage levels, safety regulations, taxes and duties, loading limits and environmental regulations. The effect of these factors on road transport operators is well publicised, but they affect air transport just as much. For example, compliance with aircraft noise regulations can dramatically increase operating costs, as airlines have either to renew their fleets with modern equipment or to invest in noise hush kits.

However, the effect of harmonisation is less likely to be felt in the air and rail markets, where the industry is dominated by national flag carriers or nationalised industries. The road market will, though, be affected quite considerably.

As road operators' costs equalise, many experts expect them to win more traffic from other modes. The West German national railways have predicted an annual drop in income from 1993 onwards of between £110 million and £300 million.

Harmonisation of EC transport regulations could well mean an increase in drawbar rigs on UK roads. A drawbar rig is a truck of two or more axles towing a trailer with road wheels at each end. However, this development could be slowed by current UK weight limit restrictions.

Continuing UK weight restrictions could also encourage the design and use of more lightweight trailers, although they cost more to manufacture and to acquire.

Demand is also growing for trailer units which can be used for European road/rail intermodal transport operations. Equipment

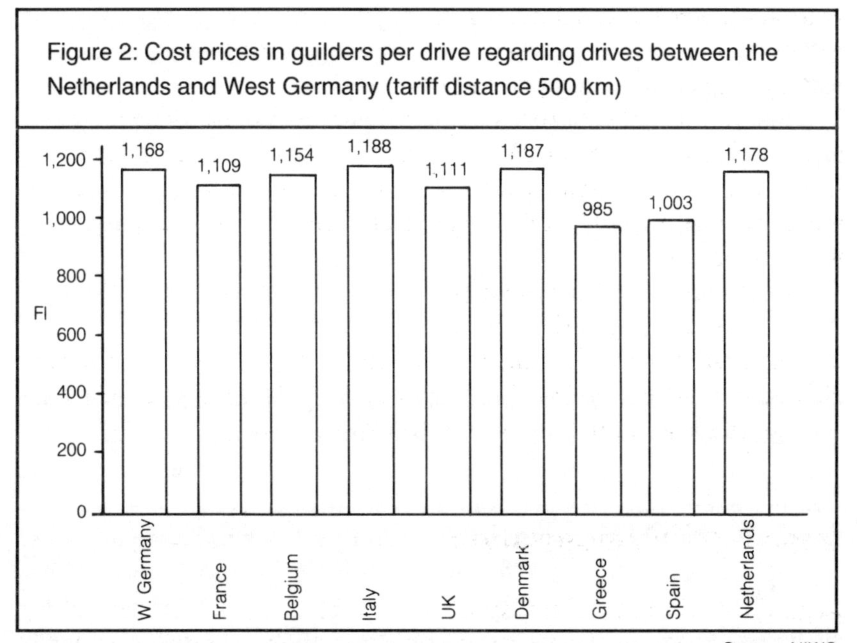

Figure 2: Cost prices in guilders per drive regarding drives between the Netherlands and West Germany (tariff distance 500 km)

Source: NIWO

Figure 3: Cost of labour and accommodation in guilders per hour.

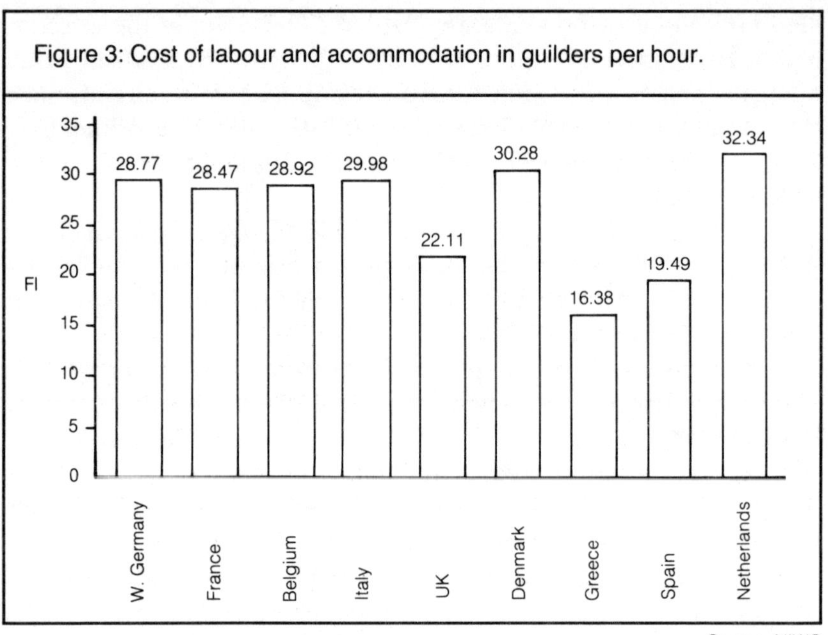

Source: NIWO

manufacturer Tiphook, for example, has recently introduced a new road/rail intermodal transport system incorporating the piggyback concept. A piggyback operation uses a lightweight rail car to carry a standard articulated semi-trailer.

The harmonisation of transport regulations should eventually level out operators' costs throughout the EC. This will mean that operators will have to compete on quality of service and efficiency and not rely on artificial cost advantages.

Several different views have been expressed on the level of operators' costs in each member state. Examples of additional costs to UK operators that are often stated are that UK vehicles are limited to a maximum gross weight of 38 tonnes compared to the EC level of 40 tonnes, and the Freight Transport Association points out that the UK is top of the league for vehicle and fuel excise duty out of all the EC nations in tax paid per vehicle.

However, opposing this view, studies by the Dutch centre for transport research and training have shown that operators' costs are strikingly similar across Europe. Professor Cees Ruijgrok of the University of Delft says that, while there are variations of costs and cost components between operators across Europe, the general average cost level of a 500-kilometre trip is around 1,100 guilders in all cases.

The only exceptions are for operators in Spain and Greece, where wages are still lower, but there are cases in other countries where operators employ drivers from countries such as Turkey and pay lower wages. Professor Ruijgrok estimates that Greek and Spanish hauliers' costs are around 15 per cent less than those of the rest of the EC. But, he says, wage rates will gradually equalise: 'Drivers will come more and more from low wage countries.' And protective tariffs and other schemes will have to be dropped or the countries operating them will lose their competitiveness.

These opposing views have led to disagreement concerning the implemention of harmonisation and deregulation in the transport system. Professor Ruijgrok believes that the general similarity in costs which his research has found is an argument for deregulation before harmonisation. He believes that there will be an increase not only in the volume of freight being carried across Europe but also in the roads' market share.

The FTA, however, is calling strongly for a common transport regime across all member states on the grounds that it is nonsense to create a single transport market while there are still twelve different ways of controlling transport. This view is supported by Wilfred Lochte, Managing Director of West German truck manufacturer MAN, who believes regulations particularly on safety requirements are not enough. 'All countries in the EC should enforce a suitable and equal standard,' he says.

4. The impact of environmental issues

There have been strong pressures on the EC from the increasingly influential 'green' lobby to limit the carriage of hazardous goods to rail or water transport and to take them off the roads. And with the success of the Green Party in the European Parliamentary Elections in 1989 the pressure should increase.

A series of potential ecological disasters in 1988 and 1989 has focused attention on the transport of hazardous goods in the EC as nothing else could. The loss of a container of deadly Lindane pesticide into the Channel in 1989 created a furore.

The international road movement of dangerous goods is controlled by the European agreement concerning the international carriage of dangerous goods by road (ADR) of 30 September 1957. All EC member states are signatories to this agreement with the exception of the Republic of Ireland. International carriage by rail is governed by RID, air transport by the International Civil Aviation Organization (ICAO) and the International Air Transport Association (IATA) and marine transport by IMDG. In addition it seems likely that a new international treaty will be adopted limiting the international movement of hazardous waste.

Dangerous goods normally carried in tankers or tanks, including gas (Class 2), inflammable liquids (Class 3), toxic substances (Class 6.1) and corrosive substances (Class 8), account for more than 75 per cent of dangerous goods transported by road, according to EC figures. Although the transport of these types of goods is more common, and more dangerous, the level of safety is higher than that of general road transport in Europe. To support this, a survey of accident statistics carried out in West Germany under the TOPAS project stated that a conventional road vehicle has on average one accident resulting in injury every million kilometres, whereas tankers are involved in such accidents only every 6.6 million kilometres.

The Commission has been considering the movement of dangerous goods by road and it seems likely that some new regulations and procedures will be forthcoming. One area which is under consideration

Figure 4: Classification of dangerous goods

Hazard	UN equivalent	Hazard class/division
Explosives	1.1–1.5	Explosives
Gas, under pressure and/or refrigerated	2	Gases: compressed, liquefied, or dissolved under pressure
Fire	3	Inflammable liquids
	4.1	Inflammable solids
	4.2	Substances liable to spontaneous combustion
	4.3	Substances which, on contact with water, emit inflammable gases
Oxidising	5.1	Oxidising substances other than organic peroxides
Oxidising (organic peroxides)	5.2	Organic peroxides
Toxic	6.1	Poisonous (toxic) substances
	6.2	Infectious substances
Radioactive	7	Radioactive substances
Corrosive	8	Corrosives
	9	Miscellaneous dangerous substances

is the vocational training of all drivers who have occasion to carry dangerous goods, no matter how small the quantity. However, the influential Economic and Social Committee of the Commission has expressed a number of doubts on this whole subject.

Firstly, they point out that the quality of the packaging is the most important factor in the safe transit of packaged dangerous substances. The packaging regulations are covered by United Nations Standards and the Committee recommends that responsibility should continue to rest with the UN to avoid duplication of work and allow the development of a standard set of regulations.

Secondly, in its draft proposal, the Commission proposed to replace the international bodies, such as the UN, ICAO, ADR and RID, with EC legislation. The Economic and Social Committee recommends that this should not be done, as multiple rules on the same subject would be confusing and would undermine safety standards. The Committee recommends that the Commission should be instrumental in encouraging co-operation amongst member states so that they present common proposals to the relevant international bodies.

Finally, there will be published in 1990 a new Class 9 of the ADR agreement which will cover requirements concerning the transport of pollutants.

In 1989 the 'grandfather rights' which allowed some hazardous goods to be sent out in non-UN standard packaging came to an end, and from now on all packaging materials and packages will have to meet UN standards on compatibility, leakproofness and so on. These include pressure testing.

It is still not clear what hazardous materials will be allowed to pass through the Channel Tunnel, and it is likely that road or rail vehicles carrying some hazardous materials will be required to cross the water to the continent by ship.

Many years ago, the UK government was involved in the Quiet Heavy Goods Vehicle Project, a concept that disappeared. That concept involved a potentially very expensive sound insulation programme for engines. Vehicle noise has become a major barrier to UK operators with depots in residential areas, because local people have, not surprisingly, objected to the granting of operating centre status to bases in such areas. Licensing authorities have often put time limits on operations at depots to overcome noise objections.

Noise has also led to many airports being forced to close at night, limiting their ability to handle freight traffic during the less congested hours of the day.

Manufacturers and trade associations have been promoting schemes to train lorry drivers in how to keep their vehicles quiet. The influential magazine *Motor Transport* has introduced an environmental award, which involves keeping down the noise of vehicles. On the road, much of the noise is produced by rubber on tarmac. To overcome that a long study into the design of tyres and road surfaces will be needed to determine any action required.

Construction of road vehicles has been strongly affected by environmental and safety regulations. Rear under-run barriers, sideguards and spray suppression equipment have all made themselves felt in operators' budgets over the past few years. Exhaust emissions are the subject of EC rules due to become mandatory in 1990, and noise limits are likely to come too.

The increasing popularity of very slim cabs to get maximum load space on trucks could well lead to more stringent crush requirements to protect drivers. In addition it is likely that regulations will be introduced to ensure that EC drivers have an acceptable work area.

There is still no legal requirement to fit and use load restraint equipment on many road vehicles. Those carrying containers have ISO twist-locks to stow the boxes, but many still rely on ropes and sheets. Rail vehicles are starting to get internal load restraints, like many lorries, but these are often safety considerations rather than environmental.

The types of commodities being carried by all modes of transport are constantly in the news, particularly when accidents occur. There are strong environmental pressures to move hazardous goods off the road and on to rail or water, and environmentalists want to stop the transport of nuclear materials and hazardous waste completely.

Some authorities have taken definite steps to reduce the risk of accidents. For example, the Cleveland area of north-east England operates a special routing system for the many road tankers operating through the region to keep them away from residential areas. Other parts of the UK are also looking at similar schemes to keep the risk of accidents as low as possible.

There has been some UK government direction on this problem, but much of the initiative has come from concerned local authorities and from manufacturing companies conscious of their image. Creeping environmentalism could potentially cut off traffic from road operators, increase distribution costs and increase prices at the end of the distribution chain.

Environmentalism could also affect the infrastructure. Closer attention is being paid in the UK to the storage arrangements of hazardous commodities following a major fire at Salford near Manchester. The inspection of premises where hazardous materials are stored is the prerogative of the Factory Inspectorate of the Health and Safety Executive. Operators could well look forward to more frequent visits from the inspectors. In addition, the siting of premises for storing hazardous commodities will come under particular close scrutiny.

Proposed links to the Channel Tunnel have come under fire from all possible directions and British Rail, to the joy of many objectors, but at massive increased cost, now proposes to build large chunks of the route in tunnels or cuttings. Motorway hearings have become infamous for their longevity. And airport developments too have caused no end of problems, as witnessed by the long-running Stansted confrontation.

Environmental issues could in future block major expansions at docks. Concern over marine pollution and over the loss of breeding grounds for birds and marine life could be the basis of objections to such projects. This is not stopping some companies, though, from continuing to develop facilities. For example, a whole series of small wharf developments has taken place on the Wash, the Humber and elsewhere on the east coast to take advantage of the growing trade with Europe.

II
Transport

5. Overview of the Community transport market

Historical conditions, including socio-economic and political factors, have influenced the development of each country's national transport network. Geographical conditions such as topography and natural resources have had the most profound effect on the development of the transport infrastructure.

The development of the transport infrastructure can, in turn, have a dramatic effect on the competitiveness of industry. Many studies have been completed in the UK recently showing how the effect of the congested motorway system has added millions to the cost of UK industry. The CBI has suggested that traffic congestion could be costing the UK £15 billion per year.

There are, however, a number of major infrastructure projects which will be completed in the early 1990s which could revolutionise European transport. These projects split into three categories. Firstly, there are those that are being financed by the private sector, such as the Channel Tunnel. Secondly, those financed by governments and the Commission to bring each member state's transport system in line, such as the re-laying of Spain's rail network to European gauge. And thirdly, those projects which are assisted by the Commission because they promote an environmentally sound form of transport, such as the building of road/rail interchanges or the development of a European high-speed rail network of some 30,000 kilometres.

In all projects, the Commission can provide funds to help development. In the majority of cases, though, the Commission provides funds only for projects which support its overall aims. Broadly, the Commission aims to support environmentally sound transport systems. This in effect means that support can be gained for projects which move freight from road-based to rail-based or water-based systems. An example of this is the 645 million ecu which it has allocated to help develop road/rail interface terminals. Future funding will be provided for other environmentally sound transport infrastructure projects.

In this section an overview of the transport sector is given which describes various modes of transport. In order to provide a basis for comparison, statistical references are used wherever possible. For road, rail and inland waterways, the quantities of goods transported (in million tonnes) per country using each of these modes of transport are described, together with a breakdown of tonnage per product group, using the standard nomenclature of Goods for Transport Statistics.

All figures used are the most recently available from the Statistical Office of the European Communities. For road and rail transport the most recent figures are for 1985 and for inland waterways 1986.

The three modes of transport which dominate the movement of goods within the EC in order of tonnages carried are road, rail and

Figure 5: Transport of goods within the Community by mode of transport, 1986 (millions of tonnes)

Mode	National	Intra-EC	Extra-EC	Total
Road	7,291.8	189.1	19.4	7,500.3
Rail	560.1	65.3	58.2	683.6
Inland water	199.4	192.6	20.6	412.6
Total	8,051.3	447.0	98.2	8,596.5

Figure 6: Goods transport total traffic (excluding transit) modal share

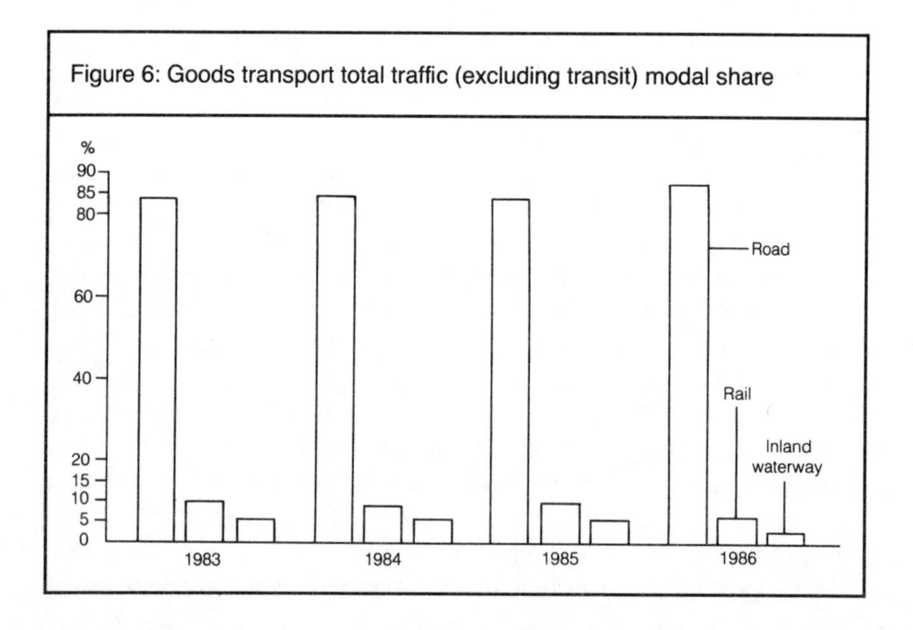

inland waterways. In 1986 over 7,500 million tonnes of goods were transported by road within the EC. The comparative figure for rail transport was less than 700 million tonnes and for inland waterways just over 400 million tonnes, showing that road transport is the most important method of moving goods within the EC (see Figures 5 and 6).

6. Road services

Three member states (West Germany, the UK and France) account for 67.5 per cent of the total Community tonnage transported by road. This is not surprising, since West Germany, the UK and France are the major producers and consumers of goods. However, for intra-EC international road transport the main origin countries are West Germany, the Netherlands, France and Belgium. Figure 7 shows the relevant share of the intra-EC market for each country.

Figure 7: Breakdown of percentage of intra-EC traffic tonnage by transport mode by country for 1986

Country	Road	Rail	Inland water
Belgium	16.8	16.8	20.6
Denmark	2.2	1.8	–
France	20.1	20.5	5.7
Greece	0.3	0.2	–
Italy	5.3	21.2	–
Luxembourg	1.4	8.9	0.6
Netherlands	20.2	6.7	23.9
Portugal	0.8	0.4	–
Republic of Ireland	0.6	–	–
Spain	3.7	1.6	–
United Kingdom	3.3	0.8	–
West Germany	25.2	21.2	49.2
Total	100.0	100.0	100.0

In terms of actual products which are moved by road, Figure 8 shows the breakdown of standard nomenclature by Goods for Transport Statistics. From this table it can be seen that manufactured articles, foodstuffs and agricultural products account for the majority of goods transported by road in terms of intra-EC tonnage moved.

Figure 8: Breakdown of percentage of intra-EC traffic by product group of the standard nomenclature of Goods for Transport Statistics, revised version by transport mode for 1986

	Category	Road	Rail	Inland water
0	Agricultural products	13.6	6.9	4.7
1	Foodstuffs	15.2	4.5	6.4
2	Solid mineral fuels	1.3	10.6	6.0
3	Petroleum products	1.7	2.7	18.3
4	Ores and metal work	1.7	12.5	19.9
5	Metal products	8.5	21.8	5.2
6	Minerals and building materials	14.7	7.2	25.8
7	Fertilisers	1.3	3.5	3.4
8	Chemicals	14.3	7.2	7.6
9	Manufactured articles	27.6	23.1	2.7
Total		100.0	100.0	100.0

Several trends in European road transport can be detected. The first of these trends is that total goods traffic by road measured in tonnes per kilometre is growing. In 1984 the total of goods transported by road was nearly 400 million tonne-kilometres. This had grown to over 600 million tonne-kilometres in 1986, although this latter figure includes statistics for Spain and Portugal.

Secondly, hire or reward transport operators now dominate the movement of goods between member states by road (see Figure 9). In 1986, 81.4 per cent of goods moved between member states were carried by hire or reward operators. These statistics exclude Italian domestic tonnage figures, which are not available from the Community's statistical office.

Thirdly, in national traffic movements, road transport is preferred for short distances. Road transport is used for 71 per cent of national traffic which moves less than 50 kilometres, where it is the most competitive mode.

For transport companies the liberalisation of the EC transport system will have a double effect. For those companies that are currently involved only in domestic transport there will be the opportunity to develop international services. For those operators already involved in international services, the coming of a more liberal transport system will be a confirmation or an extension of their existing strategies and allow them to offer inland transport in third countries.

Figure 9: Percentage of goods moved intra-EC by road, by hire or reward operators, 1986

Country	
Belgium	65.4%
Denmark	91.5%
France	81.7%
Greece	100%
Italy	n/a
Luxembourg	70.1%
Netherlands	86.8%
Portugal	100%
Republic of Ireland	79.6%
Spain	98.7%
United Kingdom	83.7%
West Germany	81.9%
Average for EC	81.4%

NFC Contract Distribution (now Exel Logistics) believes that UK operators will capture a major share of what they estimate to be the £81 billion European distribution market. In a report published in 1988, it predicted greater retailing and manufacturing consolidation once the barriers go down. Managing Director Mark Bedeman says: 'This consolidation should benefit the British distribution industry where companies have had to develop efficient logistics systems to compete in a deregulated market.'

Professor Cees Ruijgrok has conducted a study into the likely effects of total deregulation on the haulage industry. The results of his study led him to the belief that smaller transport companies would have to change and adapt to meet the needs of the liberalised market. Professor Ruijgrok suggests three strategies that small haulage companies must follow:

- Find partners in other member states
- Find niche markets in which to trade, for instance refrigerated transport
- Offer an enlarged service to their customers, such as warehousing

Some major operators have developed comprehensive pan-European networks to cater for the international distribution needs of companies anywhere within or outside the EC. Smaller operators, though, may have either to find niche markets or to form partnerships with each other in order to compete with the larger pan-European operators, a view supported by Professor Ruijgrok.

Opinions on the future diverge sharply. Most of Europe's haulage is still in the hands of small firms or owner-drivers. Some authorities predict that most of the business will finish in the hands of ten or twelve large firms. But Max Gundhardt, Managing Director of Haniel Transport UK, argues otherwise. 'Even if the biggest forwarder merged with the biggest operator they would still only hold 5 per cent of the market,' he says.

Greatest fears for the future are probably in West Germany. Operators there have strict tariff systems on which their charges are based and could face rate cuts of 30 per cent when the tariff barriers come down.

One way in which transport companies will be able to survive is to offer more value-added services. Such services could include packing goods for shipment, labelling, holding stock, or perhaps even taking title to the goods while in their keeping. However, total supply-chain management to produce lowest unit distribution costs is the most powerful value-added service a distribution company can provide.

The Cecchini report suggested that reduced border delays would cut transport costs, but that has not been borne out in practice on the freed Belgium/Netherlands border. Operating costs should be equalised after the barriers come down, but the NIWO study already referred to suggests little disparity between the costs of different countries' operators anyway.

A transport company which can serve the whole of Europe with a range of delivery services, using different modes and operating in all directions, can expect to win the traffic of many different shippers.

The backload market is not likely to change very much. There have always been backloads and probably always will be, because shippers will always be interested in sending a one-off load at a cheap rate. Certain parts of Europe are already finding things difficult – UK operators, for instance, faced with a market rich in imports but poor in exports, find it difficult to get full rates for many commodities because the European operator going home is now offering low backload rates to UK exporters. Export transport is believed to be around 25 per cent cheaper than import transport.

The competitive environment for road transport is beginning to hot up already, not just from other modes but also between road operators. Already operators are forging cross-border partnerships, or expanding their own networks internationally. There has also been a spate of takeovers and of mergers between forwarders and transport companies, a trend Haniel Transport UK's Managing Director, Max Gundhardt, calls near-panic buying.

And what of the future? A major point is that the EC free market for transport is free only for hire or reward operators and there is no liberalisation planned for Europe's vast own-account fleets. This could have extensive ramifications in two directions.

Own-account operators working across international borders could decide that, as there is no prospect of being able to generate third-party revenue from their fleets, they should contract out their distribution. That means in turn a flood of business for distribution contractors and perhaps also for traditional haulage businesses.

If large amounts of business go the way of hauliers, the distribution broking and clearing-house business would really take off. That could mean a lot of operators running at relatively low rates, but could also mean a lot of work for small companies.

At the other extreme, the own-account operators could decide to go for full haulier status and go out into the market looking for trade, able to charge low rates because they would often be looking only for backloads. And a few hundred backloads a week could meet the interest payments on loans taken out to buy the trucks in the first place.

The advantages of road transport are its speed, its flexibility and its avoidance of transhipment. For road transport operators the deregulation of the transport market should mean an increase in efficiency and the opportunity to enter new markets.

For users of road transport the deregulated market should offer the opportunity to begin to plan their distribution strategy according to real supply and demand factors rather than according to the legislative parameters which are currently imposed.

7. Rail services

In the rail transport sector three countries dominate the origin of total tonnage moved. These countries are West Germany, France and the UK. Again the picture is not surprising, as rail transport has for a long time been the major mode of moving bulk mineral fuels and metal products, and these countries have the major extractive and heavy industries. However, for intra-EC movements the major users of rail are West Germany, France and Italy.

Several trends can also be seen in the rail transport market. There was a decrease in goods carried by rail of between 5 and 6 per cent in 1986 compared with the previous year. Eight member states reported a decrease in rail transport, while two countries, Denmark and Greece, reported increases.

However, there is evidence to suggest that rail transport is becoming a viable alternative for certain industries for the local transport of goods. In 1986, 10.8 per cent of the national rail tonnage was transported less than 150 kilometres and it appears that much of this local transport was raw materials and postal parcels. In the UK, however, rail transport has lost a number of its traditional commodity groups, such as newspapers and parcels.

Rail transport in Europe is likely to receive two boosts in the future. Firstly, the completion of the Channel Tunnel may make rail a more viable alternative for the UK market, and secondly, rail is seen as an environmentally acceptable alternative to road transport, and efforts will be made by the Commission to encourage traffic to move from road to rail.

The height and width limits on UK and Irish railway wagons are less than those used in the rest of Europe, but continental wagon builders have been prepared to build vehicles to UK dimensions for international traffic. UK trains have so far been limited in their ability to carry road trailers, a traffic very common in Europe, and so operators such as Danzas have tended to trunk road trailers by rail to the French Channel ports and then put them on to the road for the rest of their journeys across the UK and the Republic of Ireland.

To add to the confusion, while the UK and much of Europe has a track gauge (the space between the rails on which the wheels run) of

1,435 mm, the Republic of Ireland has a broader gauge of 1,451.5 mm, and Spain and Portugal go even further with a hefty 1,459 mm, the same gauge as that used in Finland and the Soviet Union.

Spain has announced that it plans to convert its railways to 1,435 mm, but nothing has yet been announced by the Portuguese. The Republic of Ireland is afraid that it will be relatively cut off from the rest of the Community because it will have no fixed link and will still have to rely on ferries, none of which currently carries rail wagons.

Meanwhile, the wagon-leasing company Tiphook and several others have been developing means to beat the smaller UK loading gauge. Proposals include road trailers adaptable to travel by rail and small-wheeled wagons to carry large marine containers within the UK rail wagon height and width limits.

There are few problems with weights of wagons on UK railways, though some lines are restricted in axle loadings.

There is no doubt that the rail market is set for a huge shake-up up to and after 1992. There are four reasons for this change. Firstly, the opening of the Channel Tunnel, scheduled for mid-1993, will give the UK its first fixed link with Continental Europe and will have a dramatic effect on the international rail market. Secondly, EC Transport Commissioner Karel van Miert has announced that one of his policy priorities is to improve the ability of the railways to compete with other modes of transport. Thirdly, rail is seen as an environmentally sound form of transport which could have the added advantage of helping to reduce road congestion. Finally, there is the privatisation issue to consider. In this chapter we shall examine the likely impact of these points on the rail market.

The Channel Tunnel

'Harmonisation has a strong positive effect for road transport, but the Channel Tunnel will have an even greater positive effect for rail,' says James Evans, formerly Freightliners' Managing Director and now Director of British Rail's 1992 Impact Study Group. British Rail's plans for the Channel Tunnel are now well advanced and have changed with alterations to the company's structure.

Early BR thinking in respect of the Tunnel envisaged eight or nine regional terminals sending block trains to destinations in Europe or via shunting yards in France, where they would be split up in a hub and spoke operation. That thinking has changed with the merger last year of Railfreight and Freightliners and now the organisation is looking at combining train-load with wagon-load operations.

British Rail now sees the future in train-loads of traffic over long distances. This ideally suits long-distance haulage to the Continent via the Channel Tunnel. Mr Evans says the organisation favours either single-company trains or the aggregation of cargo for a number of smaller customers at one major centre for delivery to another major centre.

Rail's big advantage after the completion of the single European market and the opening of the Channel Tunnel will be its fast through-transit times for heavy or bulky goods without the need for transhipment. Examples of transit times quoted by British Rail include Glasgow–Basle 28 hours, Leeds–Cologne 26 hours, Manchester–Milan 34 hours and Cardiff–Munich 36 hours.

To allow access to the British Rail network, several new rail depots are being planned throughout the country. A number of cities have been encouraging British Rail to open facilities in their locality, although not all have been successful. The eventual aim of British Rail is to have eight or nine UK terminals feeding directly to fifteen or twenty terminals in Continental Europe. Other destinations would then be served by connecting trains or intermodal services from those terminals.

For door-to-door operation, British Rail recognises two available options. Under the first option it is hoped that existing freight companies would provide the door-to-door service and British Rail would provide the linehaul movement between the terminals. This would mean that the outside operator would be responsible for the selling of the service and the local movements between senders, receivers and the rail terminals.

Under the other option, British Rail would accept containers into depots from smaller users and would move them through to their destination. In this operation British Rail would take more responsibility for the total service provided.

To provide these fast freight and passenger services, the railways have purchased half Eurotunnel's operating capacity. The other half would be used by Eurotunnel to carry road vehicles on its shuttle services. So far as hazardous goods are concerned, Eurotunnel has not yet stated which commodities it will accept for transit through the tunnel.

The British Rail view is that Eurotunnel should accept the same commodities as British Rail does for movement through its own tunnels, including underwater works such as the Severn Tunnel. However, British Rail is committed to keeping in service its train ferry services for at least five years after the Channel Tunnel opens, and unacceptable commodities will still be able to use this method, although with some time penalties.

One further point regarding the Channel Tunnel is the current infrastructure available on the UK side. In order to connect the Tunnel with the rest of the UK, British Rail has had to find a quick and cost-effective method. This has meant using the existing lines which run between Folkestone and London, with some modification of the infrastructure. British Rail has, however, now published its plans for a new fast link between London and the Channel Tunnel, though it is likely to be 1998 before it is completed. This new line is not intended for use by freight trains but it will free capacity on the existing lines for additional freight trains if required.

Development on the Kent lines has included clearing them for 8 ft 6 in high ISO containers and for 2.67 m high swap bodies. Other work has concentrated on the development of rolling stock to overcome some of the current loading-gauge and height restrictions. UK and Continental research work on future rolling-stock design has concentrated on developing small-wheeled wagons.

In the meantime, freight traffic using the Channel Tunnel will have to be carried in special wagons which meet UK loading-gauge standards. These freight trains will be hauled by diesel-electric locomotives and have to move through one of the most heavily congested rail networks in Europe. However, the Department of Transport points out that British Rail are looking to invest in new electric freight locomotives for Channel Tunnel work, subject, of course, to their approval for the investment.

This should be compared to the French response to the Channel Tunnel. Massive public investment is being made in improving the rail infrastructure. A new TGV line for passenger trains only will link the Channel Tunnel with Paris via Lille and then on down to the Mediterranean. From Lille there are plans for a high-speed line to Brussels and Cologne. In addition to this rail investment, funding has been provided for improved road links and building works.

For indications of any change in competitiveness between various modes of transport due to the opening of the Channel Tunnel it is necessary to examine the freight forecasts produced by Eurotunnel (see Figure 10). In 1993, out of a total forecast of 15.5 million tonnes moving through the Tunnel, over 50 per cent will come from roll-on roll-off shuttles, the balance being made up by unitised and bulk trains. Even by 2013, out of a total forecast of 32.6 million tonnes, 16.2 million tonnes will come from roll-on roll-off shuttles. These figures indicate that Eurotunnel are envisaging the continued dominance of road transport for the movement of goods between the UK and other member states and are expecting freight traffic to move from the short-sea ferries to the Channel Tunnel.

Figure 10: Revised freight forecasts by Eurotunnel, June 1988 (million tonnes)

	1993	2003	2013
Roll-on roll-off shuttle	8.1	12.2	16.2
Rail unitised	5.1	8.5	13.0
Bulk trains	2.3	2.9	3.4
Total	15.5	23.6	32.6

Currently the ferry companies have a strong position on the movement of surface freight between the UK and the Continent. Even rail traffic has to move via train ferry. In addition, the ferries are not confined purely to the Channel. Ports between Hull and Portsmouth all have regular roll-on roll-off links with the Continent, and on the west coast a clutch of ports from Swansea to Ardrossan have links with the Republic of Ireland. In fact a recent estimate suggested that there were eighty-six roll-on roll-off routes operating out of UK ports.

Road seems to have little to gain from the Channel Tunnel itself. Trailers which currently have to be loaded on to ferries will have to be loaded on to trains. This will give the Channel Tunnel little advantage, and the faster transit times are hardly significant compared with the current transit times achieved by the short-sea ferry operators.

The ferry companies expect their services operating from ports away from the Channel Tunnel to be largely unaffected. Road operators use these routes because their own depots are more convenient for those ports than for Dover and to reach towns on the Continent near to the destination port on the mainland side. In addition they wish to avoid increasing congestion in the south-east *en route* to the main Channel ports and to reduce the total distance which has to be driven. Many experts think that the opening of the Channel Tunnel will not change the benefits of using other ports and sea routes.

Most operators predict that short-sea bulk freight will increase until the year 2000. Certainly the sender of bulk loads is unlikely to consider using scores of lorries when one ship can get several thousand tonnes of goods from the Rhine straight to Edinburgh, for instance.

However, overall the change in competitiveness of transport modes due to the opening of the Channel Tunnel will undoubtedly benefit the rail system. The major gains will accrue to transport users who send either bulk materials or unitised loads, who will now be able to use through-load rail systems.

With the expected growth of cross-border trade after 1992 and the opening of the Channel Tunnel shortly afterwards, the south-east of England will undoubtedly gain huge benefits. And these benefits will probably be more pronounced until the completion of the high-speed rail link, which should spread the effect further north.

One problem in the south-east is congestion. The road traffic coming off a Channel Tunnel shuttle at Dover would need to use the M20 or M2 motorways and probably the M25, all of which are already very congested for much of the average weekday.

Congestion is a cause of increased cost to all operators. Fuel consumption of trucks increases, relief drivers have to be provided to beat the hours regulations and regular runs that could have been done with one vehicle years ago now need two or three to beat the jams and keep the goods moving.

With the growth of just-in-time distribution practices (see pp. 115–19) in all spheres of industry, the problem becomes critical. It could be that a lot of development connected with the Tunnel will take place in less crowded areas in the UK, or in northern France. There is plenty of land and labour around the Calais, Dunkerque and Boulogne areas. The French authorities are encouraging such a trend, with the development of the transport infrastructure and local facilities. This was most apparent in the case of Amiens, which actually wanted the new TGV line to pass through the town so that it could share in the economic benefits.

It could well pay many companies to operate their distribution for south-east England from northern France. A precedent for this type of arrangement was the Severn Bridge between England and Wales, which was partly justified on the basis of the economic benefits it would bring to South Wales. In the event many distribution depots were sited on the English side of the bridge on the grounds that the quick link to Wales, and the quicker links from there to other parts of the UK than from Wales, made the Bristol area a better distribution base for South Wales than was South Wales itself.

It could be that the south-east will gain better distribution links with the rest of Europe than other parts of the UK, but that does not necessarily mean a gain in jobs and Gross National Product for this country. The Tunnel could well turn out to be as much of a drain as an artery.

There will undoubtedly be some firms who will move to the south-east because they feel they can get to the Continent better from there, but the signs are that the Channel Tunnel will have a growth effect on places further away in the UK. It is up to the firms based in those areas to take full advantage.

EC assistance

Plans for helping the railways to compete in the EC have not yet been finalised, but there are some clear indications of how the Commission's thinking is developing. One prospect is that the Commission will provide help with infrastructure development for schemes of Community-wide interest. There is scope for the Commission to provide financial assistance for research and development into infrastructure projects. One such example of this is the plan to build a high-speed rail network in Europe between 1995 and 2015. The eventual result would be to create some 30,000 kilometres of track, of which at least 19,000 kilometres would be usable by high-speed trains (see Figure 11). The plan's major problem at the moment is financing, despite Commission assistance.

Other areas of financial assistance provided by the Commission include research into safety and the building of private sidings and facilities which will encourage the development of intermodal transport. In the UK, assistance is already given to companies building private sidings where it can be shown that rail movements would replace a large number of road vehicle movements. Some £63 million has been paid in the UK in grants for this type of development.

The Commission has been providing positive encouragement for combined or intermodal forms of transport. Different states have offered incentives to develop intermodal transport, for instance by allowing road trucks to operate at 44 tonnes if moving goods to a railhead for transhipment. Some also give rebates on fuel or road tax for the road portions of the journeys made by combined transport, swap bodies or ISO containers. And many more piggyback services have developed to carry road vehicles on board trains. The Commission has scrapped quota limits for road vehicles which are moved by rail and has in fact brought a case against the Italian government for continuing to impose quotas and authorisations on companies operating combined transport systems.

The EC has said that combined transport could be assisted by governments, but not how. The UK has so far given no assistance and until a suitable small-wheeled wagon is successfully developed, the restricted height and width limits on UK railways will mean that only limited combined transport operations can take place.

Legislation on the railways after 1992 is currently only in draft form. But rail administrations all over Europe cannot ignore the legislation because it will alter the competitive framework. Certainly James Evans of British Rail's 1992 Impact Study Group clearly sees a more competitive future.

The Commission wants road and rail to compete on equal terms and

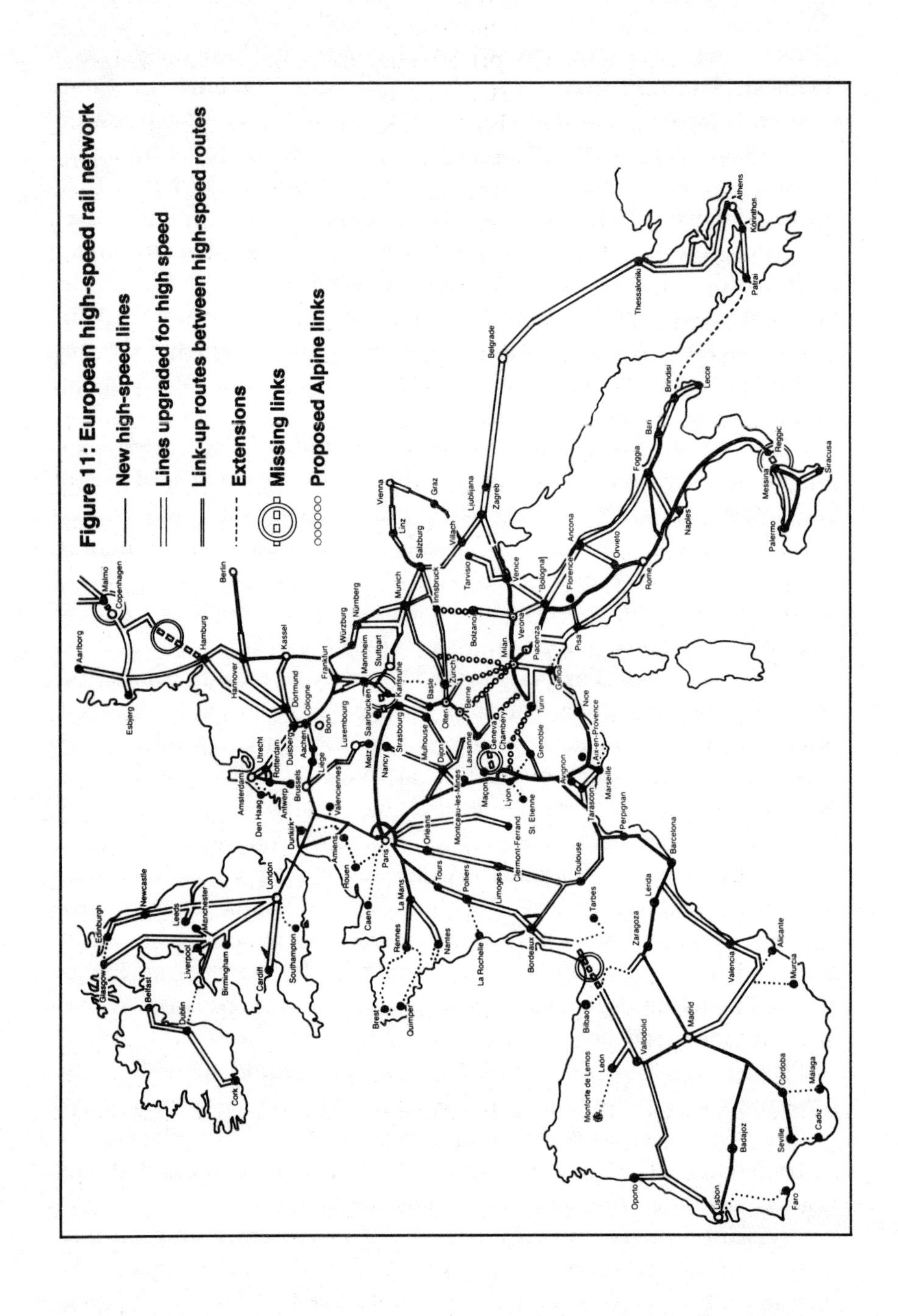

Figure 11: European high-speed rail network

is planning to phase out subsidies to rail except for the provision of passenger services in major conurbations and rural areas. This whole area is bound up with the privatisation issue and how future rail administrations should be structured.

British Rail's 'contract' with the UK government is probably the sort of arrangement the Commission would like for rail administrations in the rest of the Community. That would take support away from subsidies and towards contractual obligations to provide socially desirable services. Other services, and this includes freight, would have to make an acceptable return.

The Commission is suggesting that socially necessary services should be provided on agreed five-year contracts, while other services should be self-financing. The suggestion is that national governments could separate the rail infrastructure from the operation of services. In this case the service operators would pay for the use of the infrastructure in the same way as road vehicles pay to use roads. There is also the clear implication that the operators do not have to be the current railway companies.

However, British Rail does not support this concept, since they believe that the infrastructure management is an integral part of operating a railway. Two countries, Switzerland and Sweden, have tried to separate the infrastructure from the operations, but as yet there are no definite results to show either success or failure. It seems unlikely that the French would be prepared to privatise their rail system, especially considering the current level of public investment.

Any privatisation of British Rail could change its relationships with other European rail administrations, though Eurotunnel, the builder and operator of the Channel Tunnel, is operating effectively as a private rail company. Whatever happens, though, the railways will have to change if they are to beat the disadvantages of not having a single management throughout the EC.

A major drawback faced by the railways (but not their competitors) is that they have to hand trains over to each other at frontiers and, therefore, cannot provide end-to-end control of an international transit. An alternative that would be truly international would be to create management teams which would manage lines of route or the transport of particular commodities and buy services from the railway administrations. Joint ventures with the private sector or commodity management teams where traffic is international are other options being examined. Already, though, the French, West German and Belgian railway administrations have developed plans to co-operate by setting up joint management teams after 1992.

Combined transport

Combined transport can be defined as the carriage of goods by more than one mode (normally road/rail).

In 1986 the market shares of combined transport units dispatched were:

- Semi-trailers 28%
- Swap bodies 61%
- Road trains carried by rail wagons 11%

The combined transport service providers in the EC dispatched a total of just over 200,000 units in 1986, more than half being dispatched by the German Kombiverkehr.

Outside the EC, Austria and Switzerland are important 'combined transport countries', with respectively 23,033 and 39,650 dispatched units.

8. Inland water services

Inland waterway transport is the cheapest form of goods transport available in Europe. The cost advantage is enhanced by the freedom of weekend movement not afforded to road transport in some countries and the round-the-clock operation for goods that the railways do not carry.

In the UK, inland waterways are an often forgotten part of the European transport infrastructure. However, on a European basis they are major movers of goods, transporting some 412.6 million tonnes in 1986, thanks mainly to the developed nature of the Continental waterway system, especially between France, West Germany and the Benelux.

Inland waterway transport is increasing: 84.5 million tonnes per kilometre were moved in 1986, an increase of 1 per cent over the previous year. It is also likely to get a boost in the longer term. The opening of the Rhine–Danube canal scheduled for 1992 will enlarge the European canal system dramatically, and waterway transport is again seen as an environmentally acceptable method of moving bulk and dangerous goods.

The industry has been suffering from over-capacity for a number of years. Although scrapping schemes have been introduced, they have not halted the continuing over-capacity for two reasons. Firstly, the scrapping schemes were not co-ordinated in every member state concerned, and secondly, the schemes did little to stop investment in new tonnage while a scheme was in operation.

To reduce over-capacity on the interlinked EC inland waterways, an EC regulation (which does not apply to the UK's own inland waterways) has been adopted which came into force on 1 May 1989. The scheme is in two parts:

- The reduction of over-capacity by means of co-ordinated Community scrapping schemes
- Supporting of measures to avoid aggravation of existing over-capacity or the emergence of further over-capacity

The scheme is based on national scrapping funds either already established or to be set up in the member states whose inland waterways are interlinked: West Germany, France, Belgium and the Netherlands, with Luxembourg carriers registering with one of those four funds. Shipowners in these five countries will have to contribute annually for each vessel in their active fleet, according to its type, tonnage and motive power. An owner scrapping a vessel for which a contribution has been made will receive a scrapping premium from the fund. Shipowners from EC states other than the five principally concerned whose vessels carry goods on the interlinked waterways will also be required to contribute to one of the funds. Certain exemptions from the terms of the scheme are granted, including one for sea-going inland waterway vessels, thus exempting the vast majority of UK ships.

For five years the old-for-new system will operate whereby new vessels may be introduced by owners only if they:

- Scrap tonnage equivalent to the new vessel without receiving the premium, or
- Pay a special contribution equal to the scrapping premium to the fund when no vessel is scrapped, or
- Pay a special contribution when the scrapped tonnage is smaller than the new vessel.

The national authorities of each country where a fund is set up will administer the scheme and will involve the representative inland waterway organisations in its country in the administration of the fund.

The EC also proposes limited cabotage, whereby non-resident undertakings would operate temporarily in other member states subject to their keeping within the regulations of the state in which they operate. However, the Council has so far made very little progress on the matter.

Inland shipping might be able to exploit markets other than iron, steel and coal. Operators are considering chemicals and hazardous goods, containers and roll-on roll-off traffic to help increase their revenues. However, the shipping of such new commodities by inland water is still in its infancy.

Water has the disadvantages of slowness and is generally competitive on price only on large continuous flows of bulk commodities along main water arteries. It can be used in just-in-time networks if ships are treated as (slow) moving warehouses, but the mode is not competitive for *ad hoc* loads or to service points used only occasionally.

The Rhine–Danube Canal

The Rhine–Danube canal is due to open in 1992. When completed it will create a 3,500-kilometre waterway corridor through Europe (see Figure 12). Europa class vessels up to 1,350 dead-weight tonnes and barges up to 185 metres in length carrying 3,300 tonnes will be able to cross Europe from the North Sea to the Black Sea. The new waterway has been funded by a number of different sources, including the West German government, the free state of Bavaria and income from power stations built along the Danube by RMD AG. When open, the canal will offer a whole new system of waterway transport, mainly for bulk traffic. For the first time the North Sea ports will be open for two-way traffic to Hungary, Yugoslavia, Romania and Bulgaria. In addition all areas close to the Rhine will have direct access to the Black Sea and ultimately the Near and Middle East.

The integrated Rhine–Danube system presents major opportunities for wharves along the new system as transit or intermodal interchange points. There are plans for a freeport on the Danube at Deggendorf, and some thirty ports between Mainz on the Rhine and Passau on the Danube will have the opportunity to gain additional traffic. West German industry also stands to gain from cheaper bulk transport costs.

One major port which expects to gain will be Duisburg, which already handles more than 54 million tonnes of freight per year. Of this already more than 2 million tonnes is international cargo, and following the opening of the new canal Duisburg expects to receive traffic from Hungary, Yugoslavia and Austria, followed by Israel, Greece, Turkey and even Saudi Arabia. This traffic may be seeking a switch to other modes of transport.

Operators are also looking at the new waterway system with increased interest. For example, P&O took over the West German company Rhenania, which operated thirty-three barges on the Rhine in addition to four riverside container terminals and a partnership in a Rhine roll-on roll-off shipping service.

Overall the canal has been welcomed. By the time it opens, many companies around Europe will be looking closely at its advantages for distribution. It could also have the effect of throwing waterways generally back into the distribution frame at a time when ship operators have been complaining about competition and when the UK's network in particular has lapsed into almost total disuse.

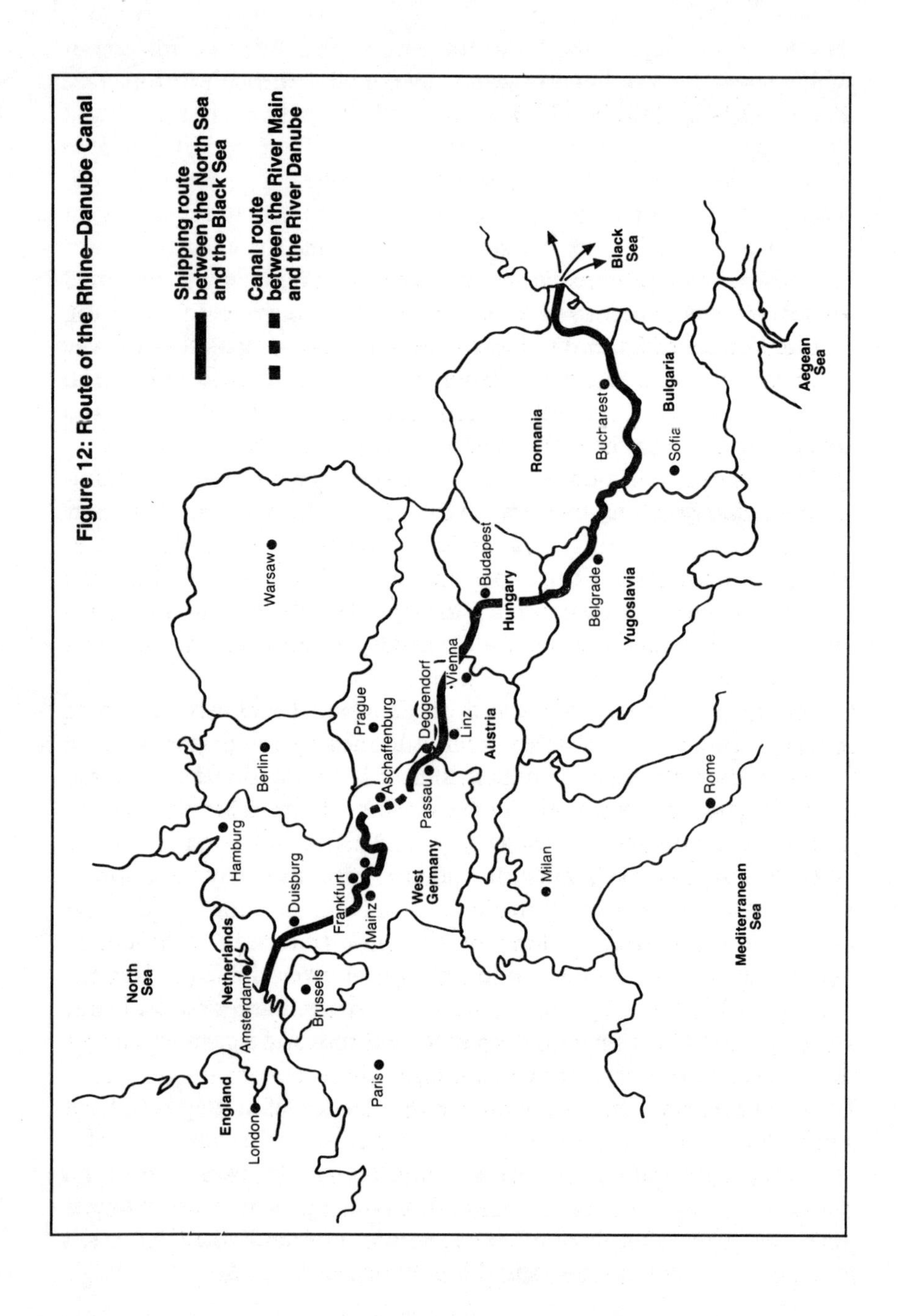

Figure 12: Route of the Rhine–Danube Canal

9. Sea services

Linked with navigable estuaries and high-capacity inland waterways, sea services could provide a very effective way of getting volumes of product to a central distribution point in many large markets in the EC which are close enough to population and industrial centres to be able to do without long overland trunking services.

Sea services have the advantage of lower cost per tonne of carriage, but they need complicated and expensive loading and unloading equipment at ports. They are slower than other modes, but can form part of an effective logistics network provided logistics managers can be persuaded to trade off speed against other benefits.

Feelings within the shipping industry about 1992 and its implications are generally optimistic and many operators are looking forward to Paolo Cecchini's expected 5 per cent increase in GDP following the removal of trade barriers. But there is some concern that operators could end up with a potentially stifling EC bureaucracy.

There are also fears that the extension of VAT and sometimes excise duty to ships, ships' equipment and bunker fuel could disadvantage Community shipping by increasing the direct costs of operation, increasing the cost to the customer and harming operators' cash flows. While VAT would be reclaimable, it would still have to be paid in the first place. That could encourage operators either to flag out their ships to other countries' registers or to buy their supplies outside the EC.

Proposals for the establishment of a Community register and flag, running parallel with national registers and providing benefits such as flexibility of vessel transfer and a limited right to enter the restricted EC cabotage trades were presented to the Council of Ministers in June 1989.

The general opinion of deep-sea ship operators is that the single market will make little difference to them. On the other hand, it could make a huge difference for many ports around the EC if trade increases between member states and between the EC and the rest of the world. In addition, the Channel Tunnel, due to open in 1993, could have an effect on the future of certain ports.

Certainly the British Ports Federation has been lobbying hard to get the Government even to acknowledge that the Channel Tunnel would have an effect on ports and shipping. John Sharples, Director of Port Policy and Finance, feels that some Channel ports could lose their ferry links completely after the Tunnel opens, as the ferry companies concentrate on Dover–Calais or the routes from ports further away from the Tunnel.

Mr Sharples is sceptical about the land-bridge aspirations of UK west-coast ports such as Bristol, Liverpool and Glasgow. 'Much container traffic could go from Britain to Antwerp or Rotterdam for transhipment but British west-coast ports would only be able to offer time-savings to North American traffic and that would be offset by the cost of rail haulage of most of the ship's cargo to or from Europe,' he says. 'It would be cheaper for the ship to go on to Antwerp or Rotterdam than a port on the UK's west coast since roughly 80 per cent of the cargo is destined for mainland Europe. Perhaps a few lines will put in a call at a UK port as one of four or five European stops but the value of the cargo would have to withstand the cost of overland haulage and volumes would be small.'

Major Far East and US shipping routes could save days on each voyage by serving the EC via a single stop. However, a recently published report by the British Ports Federation entitled 'Transhipment of UK Trade' suggests that this time-saving is not always enough to encourage transhipment. The report suggests that transhipment is a much more complicated decision, where a number of different factors has to be taken into account.

To prepare for the impact of 1992 Mr Sharples advises UK ports to meet their customers and other interested parties to put together detailed logistical packages to tempt shippers to use them. Otherwise Antwerp and Rotterdam will win by default, although Mr Sharples sees evidence that transhipment via Antwerp and Rotterdam has been falling off recently as ports like Felixstowe attract more deep-sea calls.

A further factor encouraging shippers back to UK ports could be the ending of the National Dock Labour Scheme. 'The recent abolition of the Dock Labour Scheme will probably prove to be the biggest revolution in British ports for a generation,' says Mr Sharples. 'Practices should improve and there should be a leap in competitiveness.' Mr Sharples also suggests that the Government could do more to improve the competitiveness of UK ports by abolishing the tax on ships calling into the UK, which pays for lighthouses (a tax unknown in any other European ports), and pushing Brussels to stop the subsidies by governments to some Continental ports.

The impact of the Channel Tunnel could mean that northern ports lose out. The Channel ferry ports will be looking for extra deep-sea traffic to replace the short-sea ferries, to the detriment of the northern ports. However, Faber Prest Port Services, which operates the Trent terminals of Gunness and Flixborough, says that North Sea shipping traffic will continue to increase at least until the year 2000.

Mr Sharples says that there is already over-capacity in the UK ports industry and that the trust structure of many ports makes it very difficult for any of them to rationalise or get out of the market when their business goes elsewhere. The result is very depressed charges and poor return on investment. Meanwhile Le Havre in France is looking to use the UK as its hinterland from 1992, though the UK ports have been slow to respond.

'They need to know how their customers' needs will change,' says Mr Sharples. 'The cost savings of 1992 are enough to increase volumes and this will make a difference in trade but over a period of time. There is much more scope for generated traffic on passenger services than on freight and this should give some comfort to the Channel Tunnel. Ports need to spot where their customers can take advantage of lower inventory and stock costs to cash in on 1992 and look for ways of developing the business. But if the EC puts up heavy external trade barriers, ports could be affected in all kinds of ways – the effects of 1992 could be undone at a stroke.'

What could happen is that shipowners could start to buy up ports to push out their opposition. 'The 1992 scheme will need close relations between ports, shippers and shipowners,' says Mr Sharples. Some companies are considering the possibilities of operating ships across the North Sea and up the Rhine – indeed some, such as McAndrews, are already operating up to Duisburg.

The trend seems to be towards smaller vessels, particularly on short-sea operations, and many companies are looking at low-air-draught ships to get them into Europe's inland waterways. There are even schemes for container ships to run right down the Rhine–Danube system when it is completed to get to the Black Sea and beyond, although the results of such actions cannot be determined yet.

Coastal services could also benefit, as direct access to major inland markets becomes easier for large loads and attitudes on the speed versus cost argument start to change. Currently UK coastal trade is open to ships registered virtually anywhere, while coastal trades in six European states (West Germany, France, Greece, Italy, Portugal and Spain) are restricted.

That situation should change after 1992 if the currently deadlocked argument on cabotage is resolved. Then shipping, like other transport, will become open to the market and UK shipowners should get a slice of the action.

Ferry operators are very concerned about 1992. Not only will the Channel Tunnel remove a lot of lucrative passenger and freight traffic, but the removal of customs barriers will also remove their equally lucrative duty-free sales. Some operators are threatening to withdraw winter freight services because they say the loss of passenger fares and other spending will make routes unviable. P&O is looking to franchise retail space to high-street retailers and to introduce intensive Dover–Calais shuttle services with no need for prior bookings.

But the introduction of VAT on fuel and ships' equipment, probably including repairs and building, could, according to some owners, increase the amount of sea freight travelling on non-EC ships because EC operators would have to pass on the cost increases to customers.

Kent Line, part of the Maersk Group, believes that ferry operators will have seriously to address the questions of volume and just-in-time in freight transport. It believes ferry companies must specialise in one type of cargo, whether passengers, containers or trailers. And the emphasis must be on quality, it says, with the higher price outweighed by the benefits in production continuity and stock control which come from having a more reliable service. It expects its customers to save £5 million a year through faster and more reliable operations. But it claims that ferry operators do not know what kind of new ships to invest in, because they still do not know what they will have to carry. The company has asked for the EC to agree a common standard truck dimension to allow it to plan. It expects to have to handle much higher tonnages, in quicker transit times, more reliably and with better data communications with customers. But it still wants to know what the freight-carrying unit will be like.

Unfortunately, with the threats of VAT and other problems, the EC and its member states could find themselves without any native registered ships because all operators will have flagged out to countries of convenience.

10. Air and air freight services

Airlines in the EC account for around one third of the worldwide air passenger market, and both passenger and air freight have been growing steadily since 1983. This growth is expected to be sustained over the medium to longer term. However, there will be intensified competition both in price and quality of service provided. Major carriers are aiming at flexibility and speed of delivery. Some air carriers, for example British Airways Cargo, have ventured into the express freight market with commitment, while others have entered with some hesitation.

In addition to efforts to complete the single market, which is a very important factor in the liberalisation of air traffic in the EC, growth is primarily due to globalised competition and recent sustained economic growth. Bilateral agreements have led the way to broader liberalisation, better service, reduced air fares and lower freight costs.

In 1985 a study by the German Aeronautics Administration showed a correlation of 1 to 1.5 between growth in GDP and growth in air freight volume. Given anticipated economic growth until 2000 of 2 to 3 per cent in GDP per annum, a further annual increase in air freight tonnage between 3 per cent and 5 per cent is to be expected.

There is a trend towards improved co-operation and co-ordination with forwarding agents, who are attempting to diminish the competitive advantage of courier and express services. Time spent by air freight in transit on the ground is about four times as long as the effective flying time, and efforts are being made by air freight carriers to reduce these delays in order not to lose further market share.

Air has the major advantage over other modes of speed, but cargo often ends up well away from the end user and needs other modes to get it to the final destination. It is restricted to high-value goods which can bear the transport costs of air carriage. And because of increasing congestion and more limited opening hours at many major airports, capacity could become constrained, with the result of higher prices and/or more goods travelling by road when customers expect it to go in aircraft.

Freight traffic is an add-on for many airlines, a lucrative one but an add-on all the same to burgeoning passenger traffic. Even the EC admits that freight traffic is of little importance to most airlines.

But Frederick Sorensen of the Air Transport Division of the EC Transport Directorate says that he believes a number of airlines could develop this source of income by providing a better service, thereby becoming stronger economically and generally more competitive. 'We should like to make air freight as liberal as possible since we believe this is the only way it can compete with road transport,' he says.

In fact, a lot of air cargo within Europe is road transport. British Airways, for instance, operates extensive truck services taking cargo between the UK and its European hub at Maastricht, while Lufthansa moves cargo by road to West Germany for onward air transport.

The EC's proposals include allowing charter airlines to carry freight, and allowing freight on 'fifth freedom' (see below) and cabotage services. So far the only extensive cabotage air services are those to and from West Berlin, operated by a selection of airlines including Dan Air, Air France, British Airways and Pan Am, because West German flag carrier Lufthansa is not allowed to serve the city.

Airlines enjoy six types of 'freedom'. The first is the freedom to fly across the territory of a state other than that in which they are registered, without landing. The second freedom permits landing in a state other than that of registration for non-traffic purposes, such as refuelling, mechanical problems and so on, though not for taking up or putting down load. The third is the freedom to put down in another state revenue traffic taken up in the state of registration, while the fourth is the freedom to take up traffic in another state bound for the state of registration.

Under the fifth freedom, an airline registered in one state and *en route* to or from that state can take on passengers, mail or freight in a second state and put them down in a third state. The sixth freedom allows an airline registered in one state to take revenue passengers, freight or mail in another state and transport them via the state of registration to a third state. The implication of this 'via the state of registration' clause is that direct flight operations between two states other than that of registration is not allowed unless the plane is *en route* to or from its state of registration.

Under the 1992 single market proposals, the theory is that air carriers, like any other carriers, should be able to carry goods freely between any points and for any customers within the EC. In addition to this, deregulation will make little difference if the majority of airlines in the EC continue to be national flag carriers. These airlines dominate the air transport market.

Air freight is more deregulated than air passenger services at present, but British Airways points out that 1992 is still not a certainty. If it does not live up to its promise and deregulation is incomplete, there will be little scope for the major increase of traffic predicted.

Airlines believe that the removal of internal borders within the EC will increase goods movement and stimulate trade, and that must be good for airlines. BA operates 160 freight-carrying flights in Europe in and out of the UK on European services each day, plus a vast number of feeder truck services for its long-distance flights.

Because of the structure of the industry, most airlines operate from a single country, looking to provide services to and from that country and bring in other traffic for transiting through their home bases. For instance, KLM moves traffic to and from the Netherlands and also brings in traffic to Schipol from other countries for transit on to long-haul services. The concept of a true air hub system has not really taken off in the conventional air freight market and is discussed in the next chapter.

Many UK domestic air freight 'flights' are made by BA's own-account and contractor-operated trucking fleets. It believes the fastest growth will come in premium traffic and reports tremendous growth in its wholesale air freight courier services, although this represents a tiny percentage of its total traffic. The majority of premium traffic is made up of mail.

This air freight by road market is being attacked on two fronts. The express operators are able to offer overnight or two-day delivery by air and go-ahead road transport companies have got their acts together to offer two-day or three-day international deliveries at lower rates.

The air freight business is a highly capital-intensive one, huge investments having to be made in aircraft, pallets and handling equipment. This limits the number of new airlines that could start up in the business and the number of new airport projects that will be undertaken to increase ground capacity.

There are plenty of aircraft noise protest groups and the Commission is introducing new noise limits on aircraft. This will phase out many older units, meaning more major investments for existing large airlines and a major obstacle to entering the market for new operators. Many small airlines have started off with second-hand aircraft, but if such aircraft become illegal on noise grounds, the supply of older units will dry up. Some existing small operators will be unable to invest in newer or brand-new aircraft to meet the regulations.

There could be scope for groups of shippers to set up multi-user air distribution networks outside the existing airlines, but ultimately the expansion of air freight could founder on the increasingly congested European skies. Passenger airlines have been taken over by rivals purely to get landing slots at airports such as London's Heathrow and Gatwick.

The situation is not likely to improve, because of the growing environmental lobby against noise and against the amount of open land being swallowed up for airport developments. The Commission has directed that states get together to consult and co-ordinate efforts on air traffic navigation and traffic flow.

It also wants members to re-examine the possibility of achieving more efficient use of airspace while at the same time re-distributing airspace between military and civilian usage. Already the UK Ministry of Defence has given up some of its rights to UK airspace to civil use. The Commission has also told members to reconsider the use of fixed corridors for aircraft and instead to encourage the use of area navigation. That could ease environmental objections from some areas but increase them from others.

With the growth in air traffic in Europe, airlines could potentially lose their most profitable business of bringing in third-country goods to Europe for onward distribution. People could start to look for alternative methods.

There has been a growing interest among airlines in acquiring freight-only aircraft (a few years after organisations such as BA got rid of them). There is now a shortage of air cargo capacity.

For the charter airlines to carry freight would mean them buying new aircraft, as most of the traditional charter operators have only passenger-carrying equipment. Recent slumps in package holiday bookings could change that, however.

11. Integrated services

The demand for express services has grown dramatically over the past six years and has been accompanied by substantial developments in the nature and the range of services provided by this sector. Express service companies operate in a highly competitive market and the creation of the single market is seen as a catalyst for further development. They probably stand to gain the most from an increase in intra-EC trade.

The express industry provides worldwide on-demand delivery of time-sensitive documents and parcels. Services are being expanded to meet just-in-time production component delivery schedules. In general, items transported by express services are time-sensitive in that their economic value depends substantially on rapid and timely delivery.

The evolution of the worldwide express industry has been heavily influenced by the regulatory laws which were originally designed to accommodate industries predating the emergence of the express service sector. Such regulations include the national and international postal laws, customs regulations, and national and international transport legislation. Future growth of the industry will depend on the degree to which these laws can be adapted to the unique characteristics of the express service industry and, in particular, on the extent to which national legislation can be harmonised to permit consistent international operations.

According to KPMG, the experience of the express industry in the USA (292 million shipments in 1987) suggests that there is substantial room for growth in the intra-EC express industry (5 million shipments in 1987).

Express services provide rapid movements of goods on a door-to-door basis, giving delivery within a known time frame. It does not matter which mode of transport is used – road, rail, air or a combination of them all. The important fact is that goods are delivered in a set time frame regardless of when they were picked up. This of course implies a scheduled system operating every day of the week. Express operators deliver next day to the main European centres and all other areas within two or three days.

There are a number of key elements which make up an express carrier service. The most important of these is the closed system (see Figure 13). This means that the express operator should be in total control of the door-to-door movement, using facilities under its own control. The pick-up, linehaul, customs clearance and final delivery should all be carried out by the express company's own employees and equipment.

The major advantages of using express delivery services are the speed of delivery, the reliability of the service, the ease of use and the fact that delivery times are published. An important additional benefit is that the provision of guaranteed transit times brings a high degree of certainty to the distribution function. This type of service is designed to give shippers the maximum amount of flexibility in servicing their clients. The use of express services tends to be restricted to categories

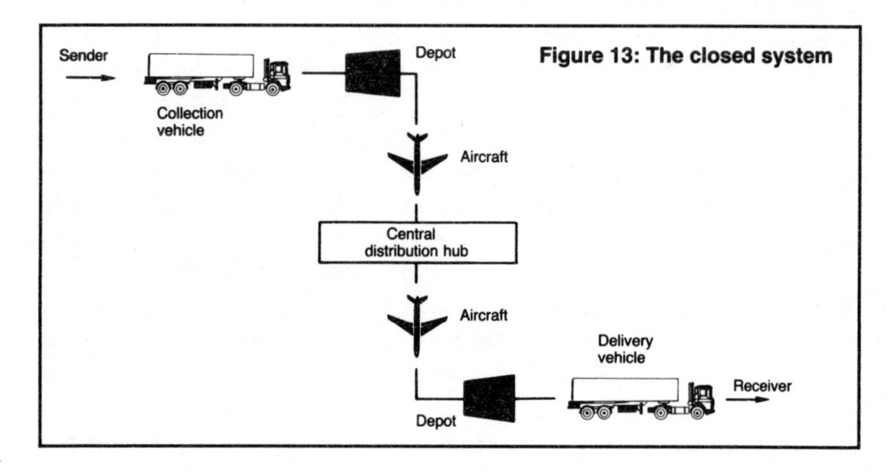

Figure 13: The closed system

of goods where the value, either perceived or actual, is high or the cost of transport can be justified for service reasons.

Companies are more comfortable sending international traffic with these types of operators because they know that it is in the hands of a single organisation from door to door. In addition, senders will not concern themselves with how the goods are carried, just with how much it costs and when they are delivered.

The approach of the single market has recently had a profound effect on the express operators. Some companies operating in this sector have rapidly expanded and developed the range of services they offer, while others have entered the industry through the acquisition of a range of small or national operators. However, the costs of entering the express market have been growing very rapidly recently, and now any operator wishing to enter would be required to invest in a depot network, vehicle fleets, aircraft and a sophisticated computer system.

The costs of providing such a service could well put off potential new entrants. The recently published survey of the UK's express goods industry carried out by the Institute of Logistics and Distribution Management at the behest of the Department of Trade and Industry pointed out the problems of newcomers trying to enter the market. The ILDM suggested that the best method of entering the European express market would be through joint ventures or franchised arrangements.

Short of the UK government offering investment incentives, it is difficult to see where substantial numbers of newcomers will come from. One possibility could be that the current species of freight forwarder will change into a transport broker, something that happened in the USA after that country deregulated transport and a course seen as a likely one for the industry by figures such as Haniel Transport UK's Max Gundhardt.

Under this system, the forwarders could act as retailers of transport capacity by any mode to potential shippers and could buy space wholesale with any carrier. British Airways is already offering to act as a wholesale courier for other operators, using its own staff to carry the goods, and this could represent a way into the market for new operators.

The growth of integrated transport companies and their criticism of the customs and clearance systems led to the inland clearance depot system and pre-entry customs clearance systems. Since then there has been a major growth in electronic data interchange (EDI), which has meant that many loads moving within the EC can obtain customs clearance before they arrive in their destination country, subject of course to any random checks of cargo or paperwork that might be required by the authorities.

If frontier controls and border administration procedures are relaxed up to and after 1992, it is likely that express operators will be able to extend the areas served on a next-day delivery basis. Certainly the European market leaders are expecting to be serving the whole of Europe on a next-day basis by 1992. This level of service will be available not only to EC member states, but throughout Western Europe and part of the Eastern bloc too.

The operating costs of express companies will vary according to their choice of prime transport mode. Most of them now use air as the backbone of their system, backed up by a road linehaul system. Changes to the road regulations and air regulations will have their effect. However, most companies in the express sector do not see their costs falling dramatically with the creation of the single European market.

Unlike the air freight operators, the express operators have nearly all embraced the hub concept. The major hubs are located in central northern Europe, Brussels and Cologne being the two most favoured airports (see Figure 14).

With the hub system all traffic collected in one country is flown nightly to the hub. Once there it is sorted for its destination country and sent back out on returning aircraft. For example, a parcel travelling from London to Paris would be picked up, flown from Luton to Cologne and then from Cologne to Paris before being delivered overnight. The advantage of this system is that it provides the most cost-effective use of aircraft and allows for late collection times and early deliveries.

The principal attraction of the air mode to provide the linehaul to and from the hubs is its speed of movement – it is the only method available to cover the long distances involved in the required time frame.

Express operators have also invested heavily in computer systems and equipment to provide faster and more efficient levels of service. The development of pan-European private data networks by express operators has allowed them to introduce parcel tracking systems, vehicle routing and scheduling systems, customs clearance systems and a fast response to proof-of-delivery inquiries for consignments delivered anywhere in Europe. These types of systems are now being extended to link directly with customers. The use of sophisticated radio systems to allow immediate collections anywhere in Europe is becoming more widespread.

The future for integrated operators looks bright. They can handle a wide variety of cargo using different modes to beat bottlenecks, get goods quickly to their destination, and combine fast linehaul movements with door-to-door delivery. Even if customs and border formalities do not come to a complete end after 1992, integrated operators will be able to offer fast clearance because they already have full experience of the intricacies of VAT collection and customs procedures.

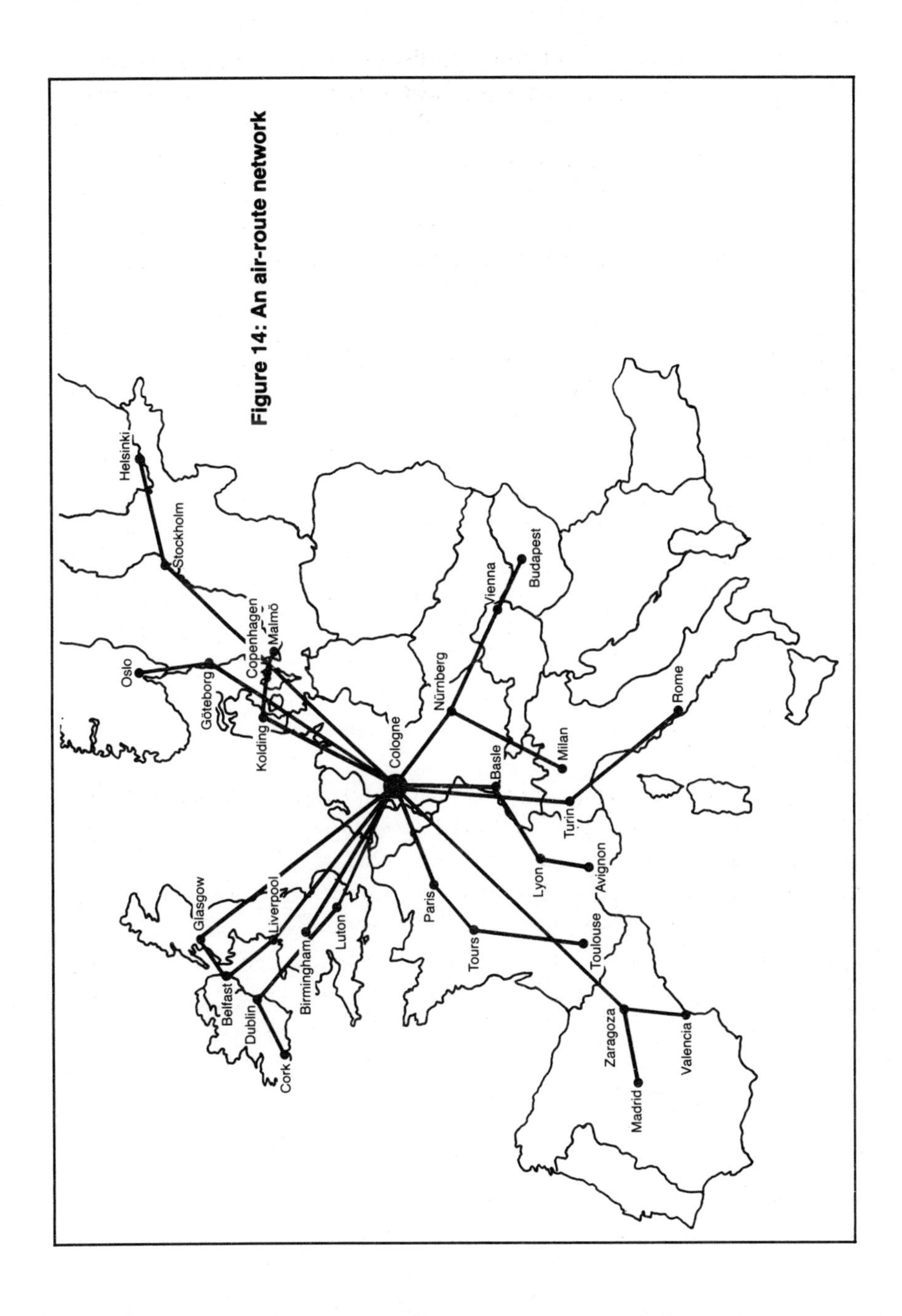

Figure 14: An air-route network

III
Distribution

12. A distribution strategy

There are areas in which manufacturers can gain benefits from the single market. Probably the most important areas will be financial savings in total distribution costs and improvements in customer service. In order for users to benefit two factors will be necessary. Firstly, transport operators are going to have to develop the range of services offered. This does not mean only faster delivery times but also the use of different transport modes and the integration of transport modes and services more tailored to meet the exact requirements of transport users. There is plenty of evidence to suggest that the transport operators are extending their services. For example, there is the growth of the integrated express carriers and the growth of contract distribution services.

Secondly, it will be necessary for shippers to embrace the concept of a European distribution strategy which will be more far reaching than simply deciding which operator to use. This concept of a European distribution strategy will have to embrace all aspects of distribution, from warehousing, transport, customer service and order processing to inventory levels. Equally important will be the need to examine both sides of the manufacturing process. The flow of raw materials and components into the manufacturing process is just as good an area to look at for further efficiencies as the flow of finished goods to customers.

But what exactly is a distribution strategy? Fundamentally, of course, it is the framework supporting and controlling the movement of goods from supplier to customer. Included in that basic structure, though, is an often critical balancing of costs and service levels.

Different modes of transport have to be assessed, not just in terms of direct costs but also with regard to overall value for money. For example, will a faster, if slightly more expensive, method of transport enable companies to reduce their stockholdings and produce savings on inventory? More positively still, will accelerated delivery help increase sales of a product to an extent which more than compensates for additional transport costs?

Much has been made of the financial impact of removing customs barriers and liberalising the transport system. In the Cecchini report on the benefits of the single market, savings on the removal of customs barriers was emphasised. It was estimated that, by reducing delays at the borders, transport companies could save between £61 million and £122 million.

Other authorities, not least the former European Commissioner for Transport, Stanley Clinton Davies, have emphasised that the largest financial savings will come from liberalising the transport system by the elimination of empty running.

Recent studies, though, suggest that UK companies could save up to £2 billion a year through improved distribution and overall logistics management. Failure to seek such improvements will leave organisations concerned lagging further and further behind their competitors. Support for that view was contained in a survey on the subject of logistics produced by international management consultants A.T. Kearney. The report points out that lower logistics costs, and tighter control of inventories, will directly improve profits and reduce tied-up assets.

Defining logistics as 'the discipline of managing the supply chain from raw materials sourcing to delivery of finished product to the final customer', Kearney bases its report on the results of a survey of 500 European companies in six countries. Almost 25 per cent of the companies surveyed reported a 15 per cent improvement in logistics productivity when measured against performance at the time of a previous study in 1981. They also saw an additional 14.3 per cent achievable by 1991. 'Each 10 per cent improvement in the productivity of overall logistics is worth an additional 1.4 points of operating margin to the average European firm's bottom line. Can there be any doubt that logistics productivity will remain a priority for the long term?' asked Kearney.

A survey carried out by the Polytechnic of Central London has shown that the main problem arising from fragmented planning is an excess of inventory within the distribution system. Simply put, the survey shows that there are too many locations holding too much stock.

In addition to fragmented planning, the level of inventory has been influenced by the level of importance companies have given to never being out of stock. These factors, however, are changing now and will be radically different after 1992.

The creation of the single market will allow companies to plan their finished goods distribution on a European scale and place their stockholding points in carefully planned locations. They will be able to hold stock in fewer places and make more sophisticated use of transport systems available, to maintain, if not improve, the level of service provided to the end user and to reduce costs.

This concept of a supply chain from manufacture to end user in a single system could help reduce costs by reducing finished goods stock levels. Reduced overall warehousing costs will be obtained by using fewer warehouses and by implementing information technology systems to assist distribution functions.

However, to offset against these potential areas of cost saving will be a possible increase in total transport costs. Transport costs could rise as inventory is held in fewer locations, because goods will have to be moved over longer distances and more quickly. However, unit distribution costs are likely to be reduced as companies transport larger volumes and the transport market becomes increasingly competitive.

Equally important to the manufacturing company will be the distribution costs associated with raw materials or components moving into the manufacturing process. The completion of the single European market will again have an affect on this area, for two reasons. Firstly, suppliers of raw materials or components will have the opportunity to take advantage of distributing their goods in a more effective way. Secondly, manufacturers must begin to look at sourcing methods which will reduce the level of inventory held in raw-material or work-in-progress form.

Adding relevance to that point as far as UK and other European manufacturing companies are concerned is the fact that they are generally operating at cost disadvantages to suppliers in the Far East and developing countries, a situation often further complicated by fluctuating currency values. To compete successfully, UK manufacturers need to find ways of reducing their costs while at the same time improving service and quality.

Customer service

An equally important area for manufacturers to consider will be the level of service demanded by their customers. The planning of distribution on a pan-European basis will allow manufacturers to improve the level of customer service provided. The way in which customer service has changed in recent years has been a development of marketing philosophy.

The concept of mass marketing a limited product range aimed at maximising total market share has given way to segmented marketing, in which companies attempt to maximise profits in each market segment by producing a wide number of variations of the same basic product. For distribution, the result of this change has been the necessity to supply each market segment with different channels and different solutions to customer service problems.

The completion of the single market will continue this process. As customer choice and quality improve, customers are going to buy only the product which meets their exact needs. Therefore, distribution is going to have to cope with the more tailored needs of specific market segments. An example of this is the growing requirement for companies to take smaller quantities of a product more frequently.

To cope with these changes companies are going to have to plan and develop their distribution function to meet specific market segment requirements, which may result in different distribution methods. The planning of European distribution should, though, be able to take this into account.

Until now the planning of distribution systems has traditionally been decentralised because that is the only way to move goods throughout the EC within the existing complex framework of regulations. The result is that international movements from plant to warehouse tend to be the responsibility of shipping or export departments attached to the manufacturing unit, while the movement of goods from the domestic warehouse to the customer tends to be the responsibility of a country distribution department.

The concept of 1992, with its deregulation of the transport system and removal of physical barriers, should allow companies the opportunity to combine the functions of the domestic and international departments. The result will be a single operation which can control the movement of raw materials or components into the manufacturing process and the movement of finished goods out to customers on a pan-European basis.

Increasingly, in fact, distribution is being seen not as a pure cost centre assessed in isolation but as a definite marketing tool, something which can give one particular company a competitive edge over its rivals. In the context of 1992, for instance, a key issue for UK exporters selling to other EC countries will be their ability or otherwise to offer the same level of distribution service for a customer in West Germany as can be provided by a rival West German supplier.

A properly thought-out distribution strategy should also result in a whole range of other benefits which can improve a company's efficiency and competitiveness. For example, greater flexibility, better planning and design of capacity should make it easier to improve the utilisation of resources such as people, equipment and facilities. Similarly, the rationalisation of the mix of goods and services involved in a distribution operation should help to improve profitability.

Coupled with greater flexibility, there should be improved reliability of distribution and substantially reduced lead times, which together should improve customer loyalty and help to attract new business. These benefits should enable a company to ensure that it continues to improve service levels for customers while at the same time becoming even more productive and cost-effective.

An important factor in the level of customer service is the geographical position of the UK. Even after 1992 there are still going to be transport barriers to serving the UK purely due to the fact that more than one mode of transport must be used. This will be to the advantage of those companies serving the UK market who manufacture in the UK. The reverse of course is true for UK manufacturers who wish to serve Continental markets. These companies are going to have to work harder on their distribution in order to provide a satisfactory level of service.

The French market is an example of this dilemma. In France, stock is commonly held in retail markets for six weeks' trading or more, while in the UK stockholdings have been greatly reduced, partly as a reaction to the high cost of borrowing money. The implications for UK companies wanting to sell goods in France is that they will have either to invest in expensive stock on the Continent or alternatively use their distribution function in such a way as to provide a satisfactory level of service without the stockholding.

Finally, companies are going to have to consider the value, actual or perceived, of the products they are distributing and the total service. While high-value light-weight goods can stand the premium cost of next-day delivery, for other goods the selection of this type of transport system may well have to be judged on other customer service criteria such as predictability of delivery.

All these factors should be sufficient to convince most UK companies of the need to develop proper distribution strategies, particularly in the light of the changing business environment resulting from the advent of the single market.

The objectives of a distribution strategy

The first important step for companies seeking to develop a distribution strategy for the 1990s is to define its objectives accurately. A key objective could be to produce a management discipline which understands, anticipates and satisfies a customer's requirements. In other words, what does the customer want and how can his needs be met? A successful distribution strategy will match customer needs with delivery performance.

That point was highlighted at the 1988 World Trade Services Week conference held at the National Exhibition Centre, Birmingham. Opening up a debate on the conference theme of 'Distribution – the competitive edge in 1993', a senior consultant with Ernst & Whinney,

Sy Zivan, said that there were lessons to be learned from the deregulation and liberalisation of the US distribution industry some eight years ago.

'When deregulation was first introduced in the US, shippers, instead of using liberalisation to look at logistics operations as a whole, used it just to cut away at transport costs. However, there is more to life than just transport costs – more than anything else, there is customer service,' said Zivan. Now, he continued, there was a growing realisation that companies needed to look at logistics management as a whole in order to improve overall customer service. 'We are not talking about just moving goods from point A to point B, we are talking about an integrated process of materials management,' he said.

As the idea of logistics management became more widely accepted, added Zivan, carriers in the USA were recognising that they must understand a shipper's total logistics network in order to sell freight services successfully.

The idea that transport services must be looked at in more than just terms of the cost of moving products between two points also featured strongly in a paper presented to the conference by a partner in Peat Marwick McLintock, Reg Bailey, when he gave an overview of distribution in 1993. Just as manufacturing companies could not succeed in the future without ensuring that they paid attention to design and build quality, he claimed, neither would the distribution industry get to first base unless the 'quality of quality' was first enshrined in operational performance.

Within that sort of broad overall strategy will be a number of more specific objectives. The first aim must be to establish total cost control. Companies involved with distribution activities must be in control of every aspect of that operation, from manpower, warehousing and stockholding through to physical transport and related information technology systems.

Coupled with cost control should be moves to establish greater productivity. Can fewer vehicles be used to fulfil the same requirements, for example? Modern route-planning systems can often substantially reduce the number of delivery rounds needed to keep customers supplied and therefore the number of vehicles and drivers required.

Similar considerations come into play when the siting of manufacturing and stockholding locations are looked at. Increasingly, for instance, companies are choosing centralised warehousing systems – holding all their stock in one or two central locations and organising distribution from that point. Marks & Spencer, for instance, uses one centralised distribution centre at Aulnay-sous-Bois, just north of

Paris, to serve eight stores in France and two in Belgium. Goods are routed into that centre from three UK contractor depots. 'Each of the UK depots serving the European mainland receives merchandise from suppliers, collates the product and produces customs and other official documentation before dispatching forward, using their European fleet,' explained a spokesman for Marks & Spencer.

However, while centralised warehousing benefits stockholding and overall management, there are cases where it is just not feasible in terms of single-site vulnerability, national presence and sometimes sheer scale. On the other hand the alternative of moving from a single unit to several warehouses runs the risk of losing some of the benefits associated with running a single stockholding point. The aim must be to find the optimum warehousing/stockholding system which fits in with a particular company's overall distribution strategy.

13. Information technology

Distribution activities are now increasingly as much about the rapid and reliable transfer of information as about the actual physical movement of goods. The most up-to-date domestic systems can already provide users with fast reports on the status of goods in transit and proof of delivery, VAT and other statistical requirements, service details, sales statistics and market information by product or location.

To achieve that, companies need to use freight carriers which can directly interface their own information technology (IT) systems with other relevant links in the overall logistics management chain, including EPOS (electronic point of sale) systems and stock control and warehousing operations.

The most significant general development on the distribution industry IT front, though, is the present marked acceleration in the spread of EDI (electronic data interchange). In an international distribution context, examples of potential EDI material include invoices, purchase orders, bills of lading and customs documentation.

IBM and GEISCO are prominent among a number of companies already providing EDI service in Europe, and any company involved in international distribution activities – or planning to be so involved over the next few years – must put EDI considerations in the forefront of their thinking.

For example, by 1992 every member state should have its own customs mainframes providing interfaces for all exporters and importers. The plan is that those mainframes will be linked to the Community's mainframe in Brussels, with the latter then controlling payment of duties, VAT and collection of statistical information no matter where a shipment is imported or exported within the Community.

Export/import companies and their carriers will have to be able to interface with existing member state mainframe computers if they are to retain a competitive advantage after 1992. EDI and IT in general will be a key feature of all international distribution activities in the years to come.

That sort of development is in fact already well under way in the express delivery business, where service companies emphasise the key role they can play in the support of so-called just-in-time distribution systems. By their very nature, just-in-time systems demand that information about delivery requirements and operations be passed easily and rapidly between all the parties involved.

However, many of the requirements for a successful express delivery operation also apply to general distribution. Areas of activity covered by IT development include tracking of consignments, general processing of paperwork, vehicle scheduling and routeing, communications, management information and service monitoring.

The introduction of computerised freight tracking systems enables service operators to monitor shipments at various points in the door-to-door transport operation. These monitoring points include pick-up consignor, arrival at the delivery service company's local depot, arrival/dispatch at the main parcels sorting hub, arrival at the delivery depot and then the final delivery itself.

In developing sophisticated tracking systems, though, freight service operators have to take into account a number of potential problem areas. There is, for example, the need to find a system which enables an item to be quickly recorded.

For operators picking up relatively small numbers of documents and packages from each customer it is easy to get the collection driver to collate and input the necessary information via some sort of handheld device or a unit in his vehicle. However, distribution companies collecting large volumes of parcels tend to find that processing each item at the point of collection takes up too much time and as a result they prefer to establish the point of data capture at the collection depot.

Increasingly, service operators in both categories are opting to use some form of bar coding as the means to identify parcels being handled through their systems. Such development is so far rather less common in the international arena than in the domestic market, but looks set to expand in both sectors over the next few years. While bar coding is not regarded as a panacea for all the problems of data collection in distribution, within well-defined and practical systems it does substantially boost efficiency and potential profitability. Benefits include a solution to the problem of limited time available for data capture and also savings on the cost of that operation.

In some cases, freight carriers are now installing their computer terminals on customers' premises to improve communication between the two further. In effect, such facilities give customers access to a distribution system for information on their own particular consignments. Again, such facilities are currently rather better developed in the domestic market than for international operations, but further developments in the latter are now coming through.

However, in that context, it is important that potential users of such systems should distinguish between those which simply tie them into the operation of one particular operator and those which give them access to more wide-ranging EDI systems.

Such considerations will become even more significant in the light of the single market, a point which has prompted the Commission to draw up a Community action plan relating to the electronic transfer of data. Called TEDIS (Trade Electronic Data Interchange Systems), the project is designed to prevent a proliferation of closed trade EDI systems with a resulting widespread incompatibility of such systems. It will also help to promote the creation and establishment of trade EDI systems which meet the needs of users, in particular small and medium-sized enterprises.

In addition to improving communication between carrier and customer, development of carrier on-site computer terminals for major customers should also substantially simplify documentation procedures for the latter.

Systems vary slightly from carrier to carrier, but generally speaking the installation of on-site terminals should enable a customer with a number of parcels or items to be collected to enter consignment details in an abbreviated form – usually the account number, the number of packages involved and their weight, the type of service required and the customer's reference number, as well as any special comments or requests. That operation can often take as little as fifteen to twenty seconds, regardless of whether one or one hundred parcels are involved, so greatly boosting the efficiency of the customer's dispatch department.

The next stage normally involves the customer's computer terminal printing out destination labels for each consignment and, at the end of the day, a collection manifest detailing all the consignments being picked up that day. The fact that the labels can be applied at the customer's premises in turn considerably reduces the chances of incorrect labelling and subsequent misrouteing, because the customer company is able to check for itself that the right details have been put into the system and attached to each consignment.

Further computerised freight tracking system enhancements now increasingly available include the introduction of direct data transmission between depots and vehicles – replacing radio communications – and computer-controlled collections. The latter allows a customer's telephoned order to be keyed straight into the computer system rather than a hard-copy collection note having to be written out. That information can then be electronically transmitted to a collection vehicle.

In fact, the development of more efficient communications between depots and vehicles is becoming an increasingly prominent feature of current distribution industry developments.

Rapid advances in the development and application of modern technology are opening up a range of new options for improving communications between vehicles out on the road and their home bases or depots. Included in that category are much-improved mobile radio equipment and direct depot-to-vehicle computer terminal links. Both are helping fleet operators to boost operational efficiency and, in the case of vehicles involved with distribution activities, improve security.

Another fast-growing area of depot/vehicle communications involves the installation of computer terminals and equipment in vehicle cabs, which enable information to be transmitted to and from an operational centre. Some systems now include the use of mobile data terminals which can pass printed messages between depot and driver. That, it is claimed, cuts down on scarce air time and eliminates potential verbal errors. A further advantage is that the driver does not have to be in his cab to receive the message, dispensing with unnecessary and time-wasting repetitions. Like radio, the system offers two-way communication, and the driver can send information to base by using an alpha numeric keypad.

Interest is also growing in systems designed to improve the general efficiency of collection/delivery vehicle operations. The first stage in that process involves efficient route planning, an activity which is now often handled using computer-based systems to help evaluate the best pattern of operation for a particular vehicle or fleet of vehicles.

Recently introduced software packages can, for example, display a map in colour on a personal screen to support on-the-spot route planning, analysis and costing. Applications include transport cost calculations, driver productivity schemes, route planning and depot location and boundary studies.

Coupled with more efficient route planning is a growing interest among fleet operators in the possibility of introducing vehicle tracking systems. Traditionally, vehicle fleet operations have been monitored using mobile radio links to communicate with drivers. That system has a number of disadvantages, though, including the fact that operators can check vehicle positions only one at a time, which means that, by the time the fifth and sixth vehicles in a fleet have been logged, the first one may have moved a considerable distance. Other complications can include busy radio channels or a driver who either does not know exactly where he is or does not want his company to know where he is.

Alternatively, fleet operators can adopt an automatic vehicle location system. There are several methods available, all using different means of location. Essentially, though, they must fulfil the same criterion, which is to give the operator control of the fleet inexpensively and reliably.

This control is the essence of IT in the distribution sector: systems should provide the information needed to control and manage not only vehicle fleets but all aspects of a company's business. The slogan 'information is power' is in danger of becoming something of a distribution conference cliché, but it nevertheless accurately sums up the whole subject.

14. The development of a distribution strategy

Current distribution methods and patterns

Having determined the general aims of a distribution strategy, the next stage is to make an objective assessment of existing distribution methods and patterns. With the likely major changes in market conditions resulting from the internal market, it is important that UK companies decide exactly where distribution fits into their line of business and assess whether its logistics activity is currently its strength or its weakness.

That sort of analysis needs to start right back at the basics. Where are goods originating from and where are they going? Are there any firm reasons for using the present modes of transport and distribution systems or have they simply evolved over the years without any real planning? The last point may at first glance seem somewhat fatuous, but it is surprising how often a distribution activity is carried out in a particular fashion 'because it has always been done that way'.

Coupled with an updated assessment of the current distribution modes and systems should be a review of the actual volumes of goods being moved by them. In recent years, for example, retailers have tended to exert more and more influence over patterns of distribution, often demanding that delivery of goods be routed via their own distribution systems and warehouses. A manufacturer or supplier may find that, as more and more goods are put into such systems, the volumes left for their own distribution fleets are insufficient to justify the continuation of an in-house operation. At that point, it would well pay the company to consider contracting out its distribution operations to a third-party operator, either on a dedicated or common-user basis.

In a fast-moving world, companies also often find that the profile of their markets has changed. Thus, a distribution system which may originally have been set up to handle the movement of large volumes of goods from point A to points B and C, with other movements on a much smaller scale, may now be routeing much more substantial volumes between points D, E and F. Does such a change in the geographical spread of the distribution system warrant a change of system or even transport mode?

Similarly, companies exporting to the rest of the Community should also take into account the nature of their customers – are they, for instance, retail outlets or distributors? With the planned reduction of border barriers to trade within the Community it should be much easier for goods to be transported direct from UK manufacturer to Continental retailer. The development of a new distribution strategy should take that possibility into account.

It is also important that a distribution strategy should cover incoming goods as well as outgoing products. The requirements of those two operations could well be different. For example, where incoming goods and/or raw materials are concerned, a manufacturer may put most of the emphasis on keeping unit costs as low as possible in order to ensure that overall production costs remain competitive. The question to be answered then is whether it is best to bring in goods in bulk, which is probably advantageous in pure transport cost terms but increases stockholding costs, or order goods in smaller quantities for more frequent delivery.

With the development of the single market, UK manufacturers should be able to source goods much more easily from a wider range of suppliers in Europe. It is particularly important that companies switching to new suppliers should develop a clear-cut policy on distribution as it affects inbound goods. Both parties should be clear on exactly what is required in terms of delivery and how much it is going to cost.

Where outgoing products are concerned, however, the manufacturer or supplier may well be paying much greater attention to sales considerations, that is, putting the emphasis on ensuring that goods reach customers exactly when required, as opposed to always seeking the lowest possible distribution cost.

UK manufacturers and suppliers planning to increase their sales on the Continent will, of course, have a clear idea of exactly what sort of delivery performance is needed to keep their customers satisfied. Is the customer, for example, putting the greatest priority on price and therefore quite satisfied to receive goods in bulk? If so, the use of normal road-based groupage services may well be the answer.

Where higher-value products are concerned, however, customers may want small quantities to be delivered but at greater frequency and more quickly. In that way, they can keep down their inventories and also meet the needs of their customers. In such cases, a supplier may want to consider express delivery services, perhaps using a standard service for stock replacement orders and overnight delivery for particularly urgent consignments.

Another area which needs to be considered when developing a distribution strategy is pricing terms. Many UK companies are now making much greater use of 'selling delivered' pricing policies, in which they quote a price to their international customers which includes delivery to their door. Supporters of that idea argue that most of the UK's more successful competitors sell delivered into the UK, ensuring that customers know from the outset the total cost of transport and delivery and also freeing them from the need to arrange transportation. Conversely, they say, foreign buyers who knew exactly when a product was going to be delivered and at what price would be more prepared to view an import order in the same light as a domestic one, thus making UK export goods far more competitive with locally supplied items.

While few people would claim that delivered pricing is the answer to every export situation, many argue that the system could be used far more than it is at present, particularly as the majority of UK exports are priced in sterling.

There are also some other financial advantages for UK companies selling in European markets with strong currencies and higher living costs, such as West Germany and the Netherlands, to pay their freight costs in the UK. Conversely, companies exporting to countries like Spain and Portugal may find it worthwhile looking at ways of paying the freight costs in those countries.

Future sales/marketing plans

Until recently, distribution was regarded by many manufacturing and retailing companies as an unavoidable cost centre which warranted only a limited percentage of senior management attention. As long as goods reached customers in an acceptable time and transport costs were kept to what might be considered reasonable levels, some company managements may have tended to concentrate on more obviously rewarding areas of activity, such as sales/marketing, new product development and general production efficiency.

Now, though, more and more companies are changing their approach to distribution and seeking to use it as a positive marketing tool which can give them a sometimes vital edge over their competition. That approach can pay dividends both for companies wishing to break into new markets, for example a UK company endeavouring to start exporting to another member state, and for companies trying to improve their presence in an existing market as competition increases.

Companies looking to develop new business or even retain existing customers can gain a major competitive advantage through the introduction of improved service levels. To achieve that sort of success, though, involves adopting a full logistics management approach to business which incorporates purchasing, manufacturing, marketing, sales and distribution activities. No one activity, and least of all distribution, should be planned in splendid isolation.

Distribution considerations can obviously be both affected by and at the same time also have a major influence on decisions such as whether a company is going to manufacture completed products and then export them or, for instance, supply them in a semi-finished or CKD (knocked down) form for final assembly overseas.

The decision on whether to use distribution as part of the marketing and sales armoury in the planning of new initiatives is a fundamental one. Customers often take delivery performance into account as much as actual price, so the promise of fast, reliable deliveries could well clinch an order ahead of a rival unable to provide that level of service.

Before using distribution service as part of the marketing package, though, companies have to ensure they can perform as promised. In the context of distribution, that means undertaking a thorough analysis of current origins and destinations of products (where they are being manufactured and where they are being sold), and then identifying the changes which are planned in terms of production or markets.

A change in marketing strategy, for instance a switch in the focus of attention from the UK domestic sector to other European countries, could necessitate a thorough review of distribution activities to accommodate likely new traffic flows. Other information needed from the sales and marketing side includes details on the precise nature of the goods being sold in particular markets. Are they the sort of goods which need to be transported in bulk, by container or in loose form? Do they require special packaging or handling which could influence the choice of transport mode? On the subject of transport mode, are there any advantages to be gained from adopting new ways of moving those goods? That sort of question may become particularly relevant when the Channel Tunnel opens, a move which might make rail a much more viable alternative to road/short-sea ferry for some UK manufacturers.

Some markets may demand high performance on delivery, perhaps to the extent of requiring the use of air express services to supply goods, while others are more price sensitive and therefore perhaps best served by using cheaper road trailer groupage operations.

Finally, when looking at distribution activities in conjunction with marketing and sales plans, the customer's requirement and needs should be examined. To develop a successful distribution strategy, therefore, it may be necessary to run customer surveys, supplemented with marketing and sales analysis, plus an insight into the service levels being provided by the competition. Armed with that knowledge, a suitable distribution strategy can be organised to support future sales and marketing plans.

Improvements required to existing systems

In order to improve an existing distribution system, companies should look at four particular areas – cost, customer service, stock replenishment and efficiency.

Distribution costs should be appropriate to the goods and markets involved. Paying too much for a distribution service, with its subsequent effect on product profitability, can be as damaging as paying too little, which then results in delivery shortcomings.

Not surprisingly, one of the major factors still inhibiting companies wishing to develop more efficient distribution systems is the cost, or the assumed cost, of setting up such arrangements. Companies planning a new strategy should be careful to ensure that any assessment of distribution costs is totally accurate. As a percentage of sales, they can vary dramatically, depending on the type of business involved. Companies which carry out distribution audits may find that distribution costs are higher than expected. In many cases this is because distribution extends far deeper into an organisation than many people think.

Sales administration, credit control and order processing, for instance, are rarely part of the distribution function, yet they have a direct impact on the perceived delivery service to the customer. For example, a distribution manager may increase freight costs to shorten delivery times. An alternative may be to get salesmen to post their orders by first-class mail and reduce the time taken for orders to be processed.

Planning a distribution strategy should involve moving from the assessment of the finite cost of physical resources, such as vehicles, warehouses and drivers, to an equation encompassing the cost of inventory levels, the sales value of greater stock availability, the cash flow benefits of speedier invoicing and the marketing value of instant management information.

In assessing service levels, the most important thing is to ensure that they meet the current requirements of customers. However, even if they do, efforts should still be made to find ways of improving them further as regards delivery times – a customer is likely to be even more impressed by an improvement in delivery service which is offered rather than requested. At the same time, studies may be made to see whether changes can be made in delivery cycles which can improve productivity to the benefit of both the supplier and the customer. Similarly, distribution operations should be constantly reappraised to see where there may be room for general improvements in efficiency. Many companies, as we have seen, now use computer-based vehicle routeing systems to ensure that their delivery vehicles operate to maximum efficiency. Others have installed modern communications systems so that they keep in constant touch with drivers while they are out on the road.

15. The strategic options

In-house or third party?

With distribution becoming an increasingly complex and specialist subject, more and more companies are considering the idea of contracting out such activities to third-party specialists.

One of the first points to be clarified when that option is considered is exactly what is meant by 'third-party' distribution. After all, a third party can simply be a haulier employed to move goods from one point to another. On that basis, the percentage of goods moved within the Community by 'third parties' or hire or reward operators ranges from just over 65 per cent in Belgium to 84 per cent in the UK and virtually 100 per cent in Portugal and Greece (see Figure 9, p. 47).

Some experts in the industry use the term 'third-party distribution service' to mean the provision by a contractor of a service which involves the operation of common-user vehicles and facilities; that is, the contractor uses the latter to handle goods on behalf of two or more customers.

The term 'contract distribution', on the other hand, implies the provision, by a third-party specialist, of a complete distribution facility and vehicle fleet dedicated to, and operated on behalf of, a particular customer. That can range from the straightforward running of a customer-dedicated commercial vehicle fleet to the operation of warehousing facilities for a complete distribution centre. In some cases, the complex may be designed and built by the contract distribution company for the customer.

Many of the basic arguments in favour of contracting out distribution, as opposed to handling the function in-house, are along the same lines as those used to promote contract hire for car and commercial vehicle fleet operations. Broadly speaking, they centre on overall cost and operational advantages, plus the fact that companies using third-party specialists are freed from the responsibility of the day-to-day running of their distribution operation.

As far as arguments in favour of own-account operation are concerned, one of the major factors in the minds of companies which decide to continue running their own distribution activities is that of the control they retain over such operations.

Perceived cost is another. Distribution contracts can be worth millions of pounds, so companies with well-established and, to them, efficient in-house distribution operations may be reluctant to incur what might at first sight appear to be the high cost of contracting-out. Equally, if a company has the buying power and expertise to acquire transport vehicles, fuel and labour at similar rates to a contract distribution service operator and operate them with equal efficiency, then of course the profit margin built in by the contractor is saved.

Adding to the case for retaining in-house distribution activities is a fear factor, with companies preferring to leave well alone when an in-house operation appears to be functioning satisfactorily, rather than risk possible problems by handing over distribution activities to a third party. Some companies still maintain that they are better placed to meet their own distribution requirements than any contractor which might be brought in.

In-house distribution may also still offer advantages to companies involved with businesses such as the bakery sector, where delivery drivers often act as salesmen and order takers. Similarly, companies producing and supplying highly sensitive goods may see a number of benefits in using their own specialists to run distribution operations safely and efficiently.

Economic and operational factors that must be borne in mind include the cost of vehicles – companies may have to pay £40,000 or more for a new heavy goods vehicle, with running costs escalating all the time. Third-party contractors can in the main run a more efficient fleet operation than a manufacturer operating a small fleet of vehicles. Advantages for the contractors would include increased purchasing power for vehicles, fuel and labour, nationwide maintenance facilities, night trunking to avoid traffic congestion and high standards of engineering to reduce noise and exhaust emissions.

The principal disadvantages of contracting out distribution requirements centre primarily on a possible reduction of control (although with the increasing use of highly sophisticated information technology systems that is becoming far less of a drawback) and the need to instigate new checking procedures. The latter includes, for example, procedures for checking invoices from the distribution service supplier and checking that the supplier is producing the level of service agreed.

In selecting a third-party distribution service operator, the first pre-requisite is a company which has plenty of experience and a good track record. Time should be taken by both parties to assess each other and produce a service or system which is going to satisfy the customer's requirements fully. Some of the questions which should be asked and the factors which should be considered in making this selection,

Lever Industrial Case Study

This company, part of the Unilever Group, has a range of more than 1,500 product lines in its cleaning and hygiene materials range. Products are delivered nationwide to farms, hospitals, laundries, breweries, dairies and food processing plants. In 1988, realising that warehousing and transport were integral components of the business, Lever took the decision to seek specialist services for the transport side of its business.

Individual consignments vary from a small pack to a vehicle load of full pallets, for delivery within the UK and Ireland. Lever Industrial takes customer orders, assembles them, then plans and loads the vehicles. Delivery notes are given to the driver. Delivery routes vary and incorporate one-day, two-day and three-day combination runs. Delivery time specifications also vary from 48 hours to main distributors through to 10 days, with trailers transporting a mix of these orders.

To service the contract and make nationwide deliveries, the contractor operates a fleet of dual purpose, energy conservation, articulated vehicles. These are largely based at the Lever Industrial distribution centre at Port Sunlight, with some vehicles based at depots in Luton, Carlisle and Bristol to facilitate the delivery programme. The vehicles can be used either with 40 ft and 28 ft trailers for night trunking or for daylight delivery operations.

The contractor also operates a satellite depot site at High Wycombe, from where deliveries of packed stock chemicals and Lever's range of floor-care machines are made. Night trunking operations take products in bulk from High Wycombe to Port Sunlight, where they are stored with the company's other products, before being picked and packed for delivery. Backloading these trunk vehicles with deliveries for London and the Southeast has helped to enhance delivery flexibility to this area of the country.

Lever Industrial Limited is the first company to use a fleet of energy concept vehicles and it is expected this move will realise fuel savings in the region of 15 per cent against the industry base vehicle, i.e. an equivalent articulated vehicle with no aerodynamics fitted.

whether for small or large users, particularly in relation to intra-European distribution, are:

- What does the contractor know about your market – does it understand the different cultures which may exist in other countries and does it have staff locally based in those markets?
- Does the contractor have total back-up to deal with any eventuality, Europe-wide and, if necessary, further afield?

- Can the contractor provide one-stop shopping; that is, is it able to offer a complete range of domestic and international distribution services?
- Does the contractor have a European system which includes a comprehensive network of depots offering facilities such as fuel bunkering, vehicle maintenance, secure parking, twenty-four-hour management cover, relief drivers, communications links and customs clearance facilities, etc.? Does the contractor own the network or is a series of agents employed? If the latter, what guarantee is supplied by the contractor that a uniform standard of service will be offered throughout the network?
- Within what time frames will the contractor supply proof of delivery information etc., and is the speed of response adequate to satisfy the customers' customer?
- Does the contractor have the latest IT systems available to ensure good communication between your company, the service provider and your customers? Do those systems provide you with a good feedback of useful management information?
- Has the contractor got the sort of capital resources and general back-up which will enable it to grow as your business expands?
- Does the contractor appear to be active both in constantly looking for new innovations which will further improve the efficiency of your distribution and in supplying information?
- What arrangements are made for the linehaul? Does the contractor own all the linehaul equipment or are third parties used?
- Can the contractor provide a choice of transit times and how effective is the system for speeding up delivery of shipments delayed by unforeseen circumstances to keep the receiver satisfied in cases of recovery or breakdown?

Handing over distribution operations to a third party can also pave the way for changes which the customer company may well already have favoured but had found hard to introduce. For example, bringing in an outside contractor can sometimes help to resolve any restrictive working practices left over from the 1960s and 1970s. Similarly, a third party can also often cut through customer company's own internal management politics and bureaucracy to produce solutions to particular distribution problems.

In some cases, a contractor can identify a need for radical change in the whole strategic operation of a customer's distribution system. For example, the operations and composition of a mixed fleet of more than 130 vehicles which delivered products from a central warehouse to over 2,000 retail outlets each week was examined. A new system was identified which improved transit times and increased the frequency of delivery to the shops with a fleet of only eighty-two vehicles. The improvement in efficiency was achieved by operating from outbases throughout the UK, using double-shifted vehicles – trunking at night and delivering during the day. The previous system involved a single-shift operation of a fleet without the use of outbases.

In addition to contract distribution, demand is also growing for third-party multi-user distribution services. Manufacturers in particular are finding that in the UK market, with up to 70 per cent of some products now being routed through retailers' central warehouses, requiring substantially fewer but larger drops, there is insufficient traffic left to sustain their own in-house transport operations. As a result, they are handing over the remainder to a third-party operator.

However, the concept of contracting out distribution activities does seem to be gaining ground across a broad range of UK industry. Leading the way in that respect are many of the large multiple retailers, particularly those in the food sector, which see highly efficient distribution as vital to the success of their core business. A major factor in such efficiency is the centralisation of supply arrangements and, increasingly, the employment of outside specialists to handle the resulting large and very sophisticated distribution operations.

At the same time, some manufacturers are being forced by those changes to review their own distribution arrangements as own-account operations. With high fixed costs, such operations may have become a financial burden for many manufacturers.

Faced with those pressures, many manufacturers, too, are therefore now handing over more of their distribution functions to outside contractors. In some instances, distribution specialists are taking over the manufacturer's central warehouse facility and managing the whole distribution function. In other cases, third-party operators are being employed by manufacturers to handle distribution in particular sectors.

By handing over distribution activities to a contractor, the retailer or manufacturer can free often substantial amounts of capital for use elsewhere in their business. Responsibility for investing in vehicles, trailers, equipment and, increasingly, new computer systems falls to the contractor, who can also be called on to design and build completely new warehouse/depot facilities.

Importantly, the distribution industry can sometimes settle for

Primark Case Study

Ex-works distribution involves the retailer taking responsibility for the carriage of suppliers' merchandise to his stores by employing the services of a distribution company. In turn, the supplier finances the service by giving a fixed percentage reduction in the selling price of his merchandise. Ex-works distribution provides retailers with a total package, enabling them to keep a tight control on the supply chain.

One user of this system is clothing retailer Primark, which operates 28 large, high street stores in the United Kingdom and a similar number in Ireland, and is part of Associated British Foods.

Primark chose a distribution company dedicated to high street retail delivery, which understood that speed, reliability and care in handling were the main criteria for retail distribution, and had the necessary expertise and experience. However, Primark needed a total supply chain partner, and the emphasis of the contract extends way beyond mere carriage to value-added controls and savings in administration made possible by the use of an advanced software package.

Primark notifies its distributor of orders by electronic link. The supplier then arranges for the distribution company to collect the order at a time to suit them. However, the collection is only accepted by the distributor if the order number has already been transmitted by Primark and, as such, is then a valid order number. The supplier completes a Consolidated Collection Note, which includes details of quantity by style, colour and size of goods actually sent. This is used to verify suppliers' invoices before payment at the Primark head office in Dublin.

The use of ex-works distribution has several advantages for suppliers:

- Delivery of their merchandise into Primark stores is guaranteed within three days, and a high percentage of deliveries are made within a 24/48 hour period.
- Carriage costs are calculated as a fixed percentage of selling price, so costs are easy to identify and budgeting and forecasting is simple and easy.
- Proof of collection details are quickly provided, with service levels monitored every day.
- Payment for goods is faster, because Primark receives the details of each consignment electronically.
- Security is enhanced, as each distribution centre is supervised by a Security Manager and each consignment tracked by computer from collection to delivery.

The service also offers Primark several advantages:

- There are fewer vehicles to deal with at its stores, so scheduling is simple and overlaps and waiting time are avoided.
- The goods arrive in perfect condition and ready to sell because the vehicles used are custom fitted for the carriage of hanging garments and boxed goods.
- Tighter control of the supply chain enables Primark to react more quickly to market fluctuations and thus improve sales.

To provide the most efficient service to Primark, all the distributor's vehicles are fitted with a tuck-under tail-lift and vehicle alarm. Inside, they utilise rolling rail and load retaining systems. Drivers are fully trained to handle fragile goods and exercise care during all phases of the operation. Collections from suppliers are made at times to suit them, leaving them free to concentrate on production.

Ex-works distribution is an ideal way for retailers to get costs down without having to sacrifice speed and reliability. The computer link results in less paperwork and in Primark's case, where the software has been specifically written, provides extensive product information as well as the normal information about sets and cartons in a consignment.

The retailer/distributor partnership has produced the first distribution system of a new generation, where information is shown down to the detail of line item number. This allows goods to go directly from supplier to store without the cost of a warehouse and thus enables control to be achieved by the software, not the warehouse.

lower returns on that investment than the customer company. By contracting out, the manufacturer or retailer can then allocate the additional capital to areas of high return.

Apart from the capital aspect, companies switching to contract distribution are also largely freed from the dilemma of whether to divert their own management resources to activities which may not be considered part of their mainstream operations.

One of the questions often asked by companies considering the possibility of contracting out their distribution centres is how they can actually gauge the benefits or otherwise of making that change. Initially, of course, there must be an element of taking such matters on trust, but attention should be focused on achieving benefits in two key areas – financial and operational.

As far as the financial side is concerned, operating an in-house distribution system soaks up capital in a low-return, depreciating asset activity. Contracting out allows a company to redirect capital into high-return areas such as production, sales and marketing – an important consideration for exporters seeking to step up their presence in European markets.

In addition, forward financial planning should become more accurate as contract distribution can be costed on a regular weekly basis. Contract hire of vehicles can even be included as an allowance against tax.

Companies contracting out should also expect improvements in general cash flow and cost control, with increased distribution efficiency leading to reduced stockholding levels. Some contractors will even consider purchasing stock on behalf of customers.

As far as operational considerations are concerned, the first advantage of contracting out involves the fact that companies are relieved of the responsibility of managing the personnel and equipment needed to sustain distribution activities. In addition, companies get rid of the problem of fluctuating seasonal demands, which can cause either under-use or over-stretching of resources. A good distribution contractor should have sufficient back-up resources and flexibility to be able to cope both efficiently and reliably with such demand.

Perhaps most importantly of all, company management personnel who had previously been tied up with the day-to-day running of the distribution operation are freed to devote more time to mainstream business activities such as strategic supply chain management, interfacing with new product development and store operations.

Manufacturing/stockholding centres

The creation of the single market looks certain to accelerate an already pronounced trend for companies to rationalise their European manufacturing and stockholding operations. The big questions as regards a distribution strategy are how far will that rationalisation go, what form should it take and what will be the implications for distribution activities?

Many North American and Asian manufacturers, for instance, have already established well-positioned central stockholding points in, say, Amsterdam or Rotterdam, from where they supply goods to all their European distributors and customers. Similarly, leading European manufacturers now often have their production operations centralised in a few key locations and supply the whole EC market from those.

A good example is Rank Xerox, whose Logistics Operations division, which is based in the UK, controls five equipment supply centres in Europe. Those warehouses distribute equipment, all spares being distributed from a European logistics centre at Venray in the Netherlands.

'Our range comprises some 250 products, ranging from small copiers and typewriters to advanced office systems, networks and laser printers. We aim to provide excellent service to our customers and have invested heavily in logistics developments and systems to ensure that field engineers are themselves well supported in equipment installation and servicing,' commented the manager of logistics development for Rank Xerox, Keith Bater.

As with most aspects of distribution, it is important to look at the siting and operation of manufacturing/stockholding centres in the context of an overall logistics strategy. At present, for example, a number of major manufacturing organisations are developing production operations in Spain on the basis that lower labour and land costs in that country more than compensate for increased distribution costs resulting from moving goods over a longer distance to other European markets.

Companies need to adopt a 'horses for courses' approach – there is no one best solution to every situation. For example, if a company is producing goods of low value, it may be less concerned about holding large stocks in a number of different markets, since the capital tied up will be proportionately less. If, on the other hand, the goods are of a higher value, there may well be advantages in maintaining lower stock levels, perhaps in one major distribution centre, and supplying goods direct to customers from there as and when required.

Many experts believe that the balance of advantage seems to be swinging more and more towards the development of centralised, single-point stockholding centres. That pattern of change has already been clearly visible on the UK domestic distribution scene, where major retail chains have increasingly established dedicated central distribution arrangements.

Such set-ups create the opportunity for distribution, stock control and re-ordering procedures to be integrated into one system, encompassing the buying office, distribution and store sites. Improved systems in turn result in shortened lead times and better stock control, with more flexible allocation between stores and increased availability.

'A central warehouse operation is much more efficient in terms of total inventory. A smaller central stock is required to support a group of retail outlets than the sum of the stocks held individually in a decentralised system,' commented the chairman of distribution consultants Davies and Robson, John Kelly.

Certain larger retail chains have over the last few years taken that process a stage further with the establishment of common stockrooms and central warehouses consolidating goods for a number of stores. The difference is that, when the orders are made up for the stores, they are presented in such a way as to be ready for the shelf. The outer packaging is removed, pricing is done and the goods are presented in unit form, in trays or roll cages of mixed goods ready sorted for departments in the shop.

That type of development has in turn obviously had a major impact on the distribution activities of manufacturers supplying the retail chains. Now, they frequently have to deliver large orders into retailers' central distribution centres rather than delivering direct to a mass of local outlets. Even where direct deliveries are still made to the stores, retailers are putting pressure on manufacturers to hold stock and to deliver to the stores only the amount required for the sales floor.

However, although centralised warehousing can in many cases offer benefits in terms of stockholding and overall management, it is not the answer to every situation.

The problem is that moving from a single warehouse to, say, even two central warehouses means there is a risk of losing some of the benefits associated with running a single unit. One of the new ideas being promoted to try to resolve that dilemma is called 'dynamic sourcing' (DS).

Using the UK domestic market as an example, this can involve establishing a dual warehouse configuration, setting up two physically separate units, perhaps a hundred miles apart, but developing a background support system which treats them as one. In effect, full warehouse management exists independently on each site, but overall it is considered as one stock.

Orders assessed centrally are switched from one warehouse to the other to maintain equalised workloads between the two facilities. This means that the boundary between the two warehouses is transient, depending on the workload. Having fixed the geographical division for a particular day or order cycle, the concept of dynamic channel selection (DCS) comes into play.

Instead of arbitrarily deciding that anything over, for instance, four pallets or ten pallets constitutes a direct delivery, DCS will determine the optimum cut-off point for that given order cycle so as to make best use of the large order fleet at the central warehouses. Having determined 'dynamically' the best cut-off points for that day, the remaining non-direct deliveries are planned for secondary distribution.

Further explaining that idea, distribution expert Dr Mick Jackson, said in a report published by the NFC group in 1989, '1992 – managing the European supply chain', that each central warehouse is in effect also a secondary distribution point. 'DCS also, however, decides on the depot area according to the workload for the day and that depot's vehicle deliveries within that area. Remaining deliveries to the fringe area are sent out, order-picked for delivery through contractor-managed transhipment centres,' he added.

In the context of the broader European market, says Jackson, the planned harmonisation and removal of national boundaries to trade in 1992 will enable pan-European manufacturers to be liberated from current rigid national boundaries and ultimately serve Europe from fewer distribution points. 'Without dynamic sourcing, the current rigid national pattern could simply be replaced by an equally rigid international pattern working on arbitrary depot boundaries. DS will allow flexible boundaries between Milton Keynes, Milan and Mannheim whilst making best use of the resources at each location. Pan-European DS can then be supported by multimodal dynamic channel

---

Cow and Gate Case Study

The food industry requires constant review of collection and delivery schedules, warehouse layouts and stocking levels.

Cow and Gate, recognising the increasing pressures and demands, appointed a contractor in 1986 to handle all warehousing and transport. The contract involves management of the warehouse and distribution of the Cow and Gate range of baby foods, specialist foods and Galenco cosmetic products to wholesalers, retailers and hospitals. The sensitive nature of the products means that the computer system used must be able to track individual batches by pallet quantity through the warehouse to the final point of delivery. Orders are delivered within three days of receipt.

A recent development has been the introduction of a new, purpose-built warehouse at Warndon, Worcester. This national distribution centre supplies a network of outbases, located in Stirling, Wigan and Brentwood, to which the product is trunked overnight prior to delivery.

The dedicated distribution centre, with its state-of-the-art computerised systems, means that all order picking and loading of vehicles can be accomplished by a two-shift system, spanning 16 hours. The introduction of the outbases allows the contractor to operate a scheduled, nominated-day delivery service, enabling a rapid response to volume fluctuations.

Deliveries are made by a fleet of articulated tractors with curtainsided trailers, and rigids, with vehicle scheduling and routing carried out using a dynamic computerised routing package.

By regarding the supply chain as an area requiring specialist and dedicated management, Cow and Gate has been able to further improve service levels, increase efficiency, and control the supply chain cost effectively.

---

selection. In other words, instead of just dynamically deciding which loads are served direct, DCS can also be used on a load by load basis to decide whether delivery is effected by road, rail, Channel Tunnel, Channel ferries, waterways or by air.'

Such a combination, it is argued, will give pan-European manufacturers a high level of flexible logistics control in the European theatre and will ultimately help to prepare them as effective players in the global logistics arena.

However, it is important to remember that each manufacturing company or retailer will have a unique supply chain and will be looking to achieve different objectives from its distribution function. In this context it is important that any contractor or manufacturer does not have preconceived ideas of the best solution but actually examines in depth each individual case to arrive at the optimum system.

Manufacturing Resource Planning (MRP)

In the 1960s, say international consultants Coopers & Lybrand Deloitte, the primary method for planning and controlling resources within a business was through a process called re-order point. That process basically required each business to define, for each component within a product, the point at which more material needed to be ordered. However, the re-order point process had a number of inherent deficiencies; for example, it would not handle peaks or troughs in demand.

To help compensate for those deficiencies, the concept of material requirements planning (MRP) was developed. But that, too, had inherent deficiencies; for instance, it was not linked directly to the market place through forecasting and therefore was not reactive to changes in demands.

As a result, the 1970s saw the development of the MRPII philosophy which is defined as 'a method for the effective planning of all resources of a manufacturing company, resources including materials, labour, machines and money'. Elaborating on that definition, Coopers and Lybrand Deloitte say:

> MRPII is a closed loop system which links together long range planning, sales and operations planning, forecasting, master production scheduling, material requirements planning, capacity requirements planning, purchasing and cost accounting. By integrating the commercial, manufacturing and financial aspects of the business, major benefits can be achieved.

Included in those benefits are a reduction in inventory; by linking the forecast to the production planning and MRP process, the correct material can be ordered to meet market demand. At the same time, companies can increase asset utilisation through better planning techniques.

Distribution Resource Planning (DRP)

Defined as 'the process of planning the key resources within a distribution system including warehouse space, manpower trucks and inventory', DRP is similar in concept to MRPII.

To implement the principles and practises of DRP, say Coopers & Lybrand Deloitte, a business must first define its distribution network, including the definition of supply points (where finished goods will come from), the regional distribution centres (RDCs) and local distribution centres (depots).

In addition to defining the distribution network the business must determine the forecast of demand and the lead time between each point in the network. The forecast must drive out from the depots, with each of those forecasts being consolidated at the supply point. The resulting total of forecasted demand for the complete distribution network can then be used to create the production programme. Coopers & Lybrand Deloitte explain:

> Once the distribution network has been established, forecasts generated and lead times defined, DRP can be used to plan and execute replenishment orders.
>
> DRP works in a very similar way to MRP. It looks at the forecast or current customer orders at the lowest point in the distribution network, for example the depot subtracts the current stock on hand at the depot and any open replenishment orders.
>
> From this, DRP can calculate the total net requirements for the depot. Once the net requirements are generated, then they are offset for the lead time between the RDC and the depot and a suggested replenishment order is generated. This process is then replicated for the next level in the distribution network.
>
> Through the use of DRP, we have better visibility into when shipments are required and when materials will be received. Utilising this information, we can plan other resources within the warehouse such as the number of forklift trucks required, pallet spaces and personnel. The information can also be used to assist vehicle transport planning.

Alan Waller, Senior Logistics Partner with Coopers & Lybrand Deloitte, and Dean of the Faculty of Freight of the Chartered Institute of Transport, comments on the development and impact of MRP/DRP in a European environment:

> For any European organisation the ultimate business objective must be to achieve increased customer responsiveness at a lower total delivered cost. Information technology is the key enabler in supporting integrated manufacturing and distribution planning to achieve operational integration and visibility of information. This will need to be across functions, across borders, and where appropriate across supply chain partners.

Final delivery

Another important factor which should always be taken into account when developing a distribution strategy – and even more so with the advent of the single market – is the structure of the export sales network. Are goods shipped to an agent, a distributor or end user, or perhaps to another part of the same group as the exporter? The identity and nature of the final receiver could well have a significant bearing on the planning and execution of a company's overall distribution strategy.

If products are being distributed through an agent, larger quantities will be delivered to a single point – delivery will be made in bulk for the international leg of the journey and the agent will then handle the inland movement of goods to distributors or end users. But if deliveries are being made to distributors, companies are probably going to require something between a bulk and part load, depending on the nature of the goods or products involved.

However, with the removal of frontier barriers to trade associated with the creation of the single market, UK companies involved in exporting to other European countries are likely increasingly to distribute their goods directly to retail outlets and end users. If the company's export sales strategy includes selling directly to end users, there will be a greater call for the movement of smaller shipments, perhaps including spare parts or components back-up, to a greater number of points.

In the past, taking the end-user route involved running greater risks in terms of distribution system development and growing market share. This was due in part to the fact that until recently a single pan-European door-to-door delivery system under the control of a single efficient transport organisation did not exist. However, the mid-1980s saw the development of integrated door-to-door services which have allowed companies to change their export sales structure and begin selling directly to end users.

In addition to customers, distribution systems are also increasingly having to include the movement of goods between different parts of the same organisation. Large multinational manufacturing concerns now tend to consolidate the manufacture of specific products at a single specialised production plant serving the whole of Europe. At the same time, they are also likely to move large volumes of components, semi-finished goods and spare parts between different locations around Europe.

In the run up to the year 2000 the market for integrated door-to-door pan-European express delivery services serving the needs of exporters supplying end users directly from single warehouse locations will be among the fastest growing transport markets in the world. Some of the benefits of selling directly to end users include:

- Increased sales derived from a direct interface with the end user
- Avoidance of distributor's 'middle-man' profit margins
- Reduction of intermediate distribution points
- Uniform product image through application of consistent marketing policies across the whole of Europe
- Reduction of working capital through improved cash flow
- Elimination of the risk of having all the eggs in one distributor's basket
- Improved control of customer service

There are of course many other benefits. In practice, though, the decision to sell through distributors or direct to end users tends to be taken on an industry-by-industry basis. General guidelines would suggest that unless there are financial benefits to be derived from combining the use of a shared distribution system it pays to investigate setting up a company-owned direct sales organisation in export markets to interface directly with end users.

For example, the distribution of newspapers is handled across Europe by wholesalers who combine titles produced by different publishers for simultaneous delivery to 'end user' retail newsagents. It does not make sense for individual publishers to operate solus distribution systems, which would destroy the economies of scale which exist in the long-established wholesaling network. 'Increasing the cost of newspaper distribution would result in increases in newspaper prices and a consequent decline in circulation and readership,' says Chris Haslam, Circulation Director of the *Daily Telegraph*.

On the other hand it does not make sense to use a distributor for selling computers in export markets – a middle man will not be inclined to devote the same attention to detail as would the manufacturer in attempting to build up sales. Furthermore, distribution cost advantages cannot be derived from delivering computers to solus product sales outlets in quite the same way as they can from delivering newspapers. Accordingly many computer manufacturers employ direct sales organisation in export markets selling to end users.

IV
Implementation

16. Just-in-time distribution

The last few years have seen a major move towards the adoption of just-in-time (JIT) distribution and inventory systems. JIT is exactly what its name suggests. The idea is that a distribution system is established whereby goods arrive at their appointed destination at a specific time – the inference being that arrival even just a few minutes late or early will be unacceptable.

The principle of JIT was originally developed to reduce stocks of finished goods and to allow manufacturers to be more responsive to market demands. This concept developed through the entire manufacturing process and now encompasses the whole supply chain, from ordering of raw materials and components for manufacturing to delivery of finished goods to the sales organisation.

This concept has had a significant number of implications for all areas of a company. Firstly, because the basis of any manufacturing programme is the sales forecast of number of units, models, etc., companies ensure that the sales organisation takes responsibility for their predictions by 'selling' the finished goods to the sales organisation. This has ensured that sales forecasts have become more accurate.

Secondly, as companies have become more responsive to market demands they have had to produce smaller batch sizes and be more responsive on model types produced in each batch. For example, a leading Japanese car manufacturer claims to be able to produce any specific model from any specific batch.

Thirdly, as batch sizes are reduced and more flexibility is built in to the manufacturing process, pressure has been put on the supply of incoming raw materials and components. To cope with this increased pressure, manufacturers have either had to hold a much larger stock of raw materials or move over to full JIT systems.

UK manufacturing companies seeking to reduce stockholding costs and at the same time improve delivery service to customers on the continent may well benefit from adopting the just-in-time concept as an integral part of their overall distribution strategy.

JIT is in fact increasingly seen as a key factor in the development of truly global manufacturing operations, many of which now involve

Newsfast Case Study

The newspaper business is an extremely time-sensitive industry and delays of hours and, in some cases, minutes can have a dramatic effect on deadlines and, consequently a newspaper's credibility and popularity. The principals of 'Just in Time' apply here as much as in any other industry.

The decision by a major newspaper publisher back in 1986 to move delivery away from the traditional, multi-user rail method and onto the road led to a revolution in newspaper distribution. Using rail for distribution, newspaper bundles had been individually labelled by destination, despite the fact that all newspapers on the train were the same edition, and wholesalers used to have to collect from stations. By moving delivery onto the road, the contractors could introduce a system whereby all the bundles of newspapers are counted, and the total consignment delivered to the distination. Wholesalers now receive deliveries direct.

Delivery performance is monitored and recorded daily on computer systems, where real time on screen access to relevant information is available at the push of a button. Daily reports are supplied to the customer, along with weekly report summaries. Time sensitivity is the hallmark of the operation: if the distribution function fails, that day's newspaper is dead.

The advantage that road delivery has over rail has also been well illustrated during times of crisis. With newspapers buzzing with the latest news of a crisis and special editions quite normal practice, trucks can be on standby whilst rail timetables prevent trains being able to provide an adequate service.

The new era in newspaper distribution has given the publisher total control of the situation. He now has the flexibility to control the number of editions he wants to get out and to use the print centres most convenient and suitable to his needs – all because he has control of the transport.

major multinational companies shipping parts and semi-finished products between subsidiaries around the world for final assembly or distribution. About one third of international trade is now reckoned to be intra-company, with parts sometimes moving four or five times before final assembly.

Such systems are normally receiver-driven, with the consignee dictating when goods should be delivered and in what quantities. That fits in with the general pattern of distribution industry development as demonstrated in the UK domestic market, where the major retailers have in recent years increasingly used massive buying power to put pressure on manufacturers and suppliers to deliver exactly according to their requirements.

Manufacturers themselves can use JIT to make their own businesses more efficient by putting pressure on their suppliers of raw materials or components to deliver them in smaller but more frequent quantities 'just in time' to meet production requirements. Although, to date, the main practitioners of JIT are large multinational organisations, there is no good reason why the concept should not also be adopted in some form by smaller manufacturers, although they may lack the purchasing power of their larger rivals to put pressure on suppliers.

A key factor in the success or otherwise of a JIT system – and any other distribution operation – is good communication between the supplier, transport service provider and customers. Detailed discussions should be held prior to development of a distribution system to discover what is necessary and practical. It goes without saying that such communication should also continue once the operation is up and running so that problem areas can be spotlighted early on and solutions developed as quickly as possible.

JIT generally works best when it involves the distribution of a limited number of products. It is very difficult to operate a successful JIT system where thousands of different products are being shipped. However, the more industries standardise products, as the automotive industry, for example, is now doing, the more feasible it is to maintain a JIT approach to distribution strategy.

Fundamentally, it comes down to a question of gearing manufacturing and distribution to market needs as opposed to production requirements. Before JIT was widely accepted, manufacturing was all about production costs and production variances, whereas now manufacturing performance is increasingly being measured against customer demand.

Coupled with efforts to reduce the number of different product ranges being distributed should be a move to cut down the number of suppliers. One obvious way to weed out the number is to find out which suppliers are willing and able to respond to the demand of a JIT system and which are unwilling or unable to do so. Many large manufacturing organisations have over the last few years progressively reduced their sources of supply to a few principal vendors, with whom they have established a genuine business partnership.

In that context, before implementing a JIT system, companies should also make a close study not only of how many suppliers they have but also where they are located. With the likelihood that the internal market will open up new opportunities for international sourcing of goods, the rationalisation of suppliers becomes even more important. In some cases that process is already well advanced. A number of major manufacturing organisations, for example, have taken the idea a significant stage further by using their buying power to encourage suppliers to open up new locations close to their manufacturing bases.

Having rationalised the range of goods being handled through a distribution system and the number of suppliers involved, the next logical step is to extend the same exercise to the receiving points. Manufacturers may find advantages, for instance, in developing one central stockholding point for all incoming goods and then distributing them out from there to individual production plants. Retailers in the UK have already gone a long way down the path with the establishment of massive central distribution centres which cover retail outlets over a large area.

Illustrating once again the point that distribution has to be considered in the light of an overall logistics management approach, assessment of the best set-up for receiving incoming suppliers may lead companies to consider whether it might be advantageous to close down, for instance, three separate manufacturing plants and consolidate all production on one site, thus creating a single point of reception for all incoming goods.

Once the basic framework of the distribution operation is established, the next stage in the implementation of a system should involve looking at the requirements of particular product lines. In a manufacturing operation, for example, it may be necessary to devise order cycles for some components which involve daily deliveries while others require only a weekly delivery. Similarly, a thorough analysis should be made to determine the best mode of transport for individual product lines.

Then comes the big decision whether to handle distribution activities in-house or through a third-party contractor. If the in-house option is taken, areas which should be addressed include ways of improving the utilisation of facilities and people, the focusing of resources on areas where they can have most impact, rationalising activities to eliminate any drains on profitability, the identification and understanding of business cycles to improve distribution planning, improved delivery reliability to increase customer satisfaction and loyalty and the reduction of lead times to improve market performance and lessen the impact of unexpected developments.

The main advantages of adopting a JIT system revolve around cost savings through reduced inventory levels, reduced finished goods stocks, reduced handling costs and better customer service. Reduced inventory levels and capital outlay can be achieved through JIT by taking delivery only of small quantities of goods on a more frequent basis and eliminating stockholding at the manufacturing plant.

Other benefits from this arrangement include cost savings in hand-

Rover Case Study

In 1987 Rover Group identified its new model programme for the Longbridge site. At the time, Longbridge had a production facility with two assembly lines running down the inside of the building, separated by a stock-holding facility in the centre.

In order to introduce the new models, Rover decided to move the stockholding out of its position between the two assembly lines to a new, dedicated warehouse facility at Wythall, some 15 minutes away by road. The Group also decided to introduce the JIT concept to Longbridge and nominated a distribution partner to help it set up and run the new operation. This action allowed Rover to introduce one new production line down the centre of the plant for the assembly of the Rover 200/400 series vehicles and Honda Concerto.

The 100,000 square foot warehouse at Wythall handles a significant proportion of the components destined for this production line, together with those components destined for the Mini and Metro lines. Rover's distribution partner is responsible for managing the Wythall distribution centre and for feeding these components and assemblies direct to the production lines, to tight and controlled scales.

Deliveries by suppliers are made to the site to strict time schedules. Product is then received, checked, located and stored in racking using a high bay, narrow aisle racking system, with the assistance of a sophisticated computer back-up system.

To enhance JIT function, the two companies jointly designed and developed a system of connected trolleys which accommodate pallets and stillages in current use. The distribution company then worked with Rover on the design of a specialised trailer which locates the resulting trolleys within a system of fixed guide rails. The end result is the very rapid off-loading of full containers and the reloading of empties at Longbridge. The typical time taken to discharge a full 40 ft trailer is two minutes, where normally a trailer can take up to half an hour to unload. The 'trains' then take the parts to the nearest receiving point to the workstation requiring the material.

The introduction of this method has helped Rover to support its intention of building a car at a rate of one a minute where, traditionally, it had only built cars at an average rate of 34 an hour. Within 12 months, the JIT programme had helped Rover Group to increase its production efficiency. Since it began, the Rover contract has been consistently subjected to a proactive programme of development. The systems originally developed have been upgraded, as have the procedures for goods receipt, storage and dispatch. Methods of handling have also been improved.

Such continual reviews have enabled Rover Group to become 'leaner and fitter', and have also resulted in a much more cost-efficient operation.

ling production parts as they are delivered in order ready for the assembly line from the distribution centre, and increased supplier discipline. Increased supplier discipline has meant that components are delivered as they are required in correct batch sizes and that parts are always available for the assembly line. The absence of any part at the correct time could cause a production stoppage which might be very costly.

Suppliers to the large assembly plants have often seen the imposition of JIT systems as causing an increase in their costs, since they are now responsible for holding stocks of goods for the manufacturers. However, there is no reason why the suppliers cannot in turn develop their own JIT systems to reduce these costs and in the process make themselves more competitive.

The concept of JIT has rapidly become accepted by a large number of manufacturing companies. However, just-in-time distribution is only part of a much wider concept which has encompassed all areas of a company. The success of any JIT system, however, depends to a large extent on the way in which the suppliers, manufacturers and any contractor work together to build a long relationship. The financial advantages to the manufacturer can be great, and suppliers could use the imposition of a JIT system to improve their own competitiveness.

17. Express distribution

UK companies looking to overcome the disadvantages of geography and the English Channel in developing export sales on the Continent should consider using express distribution services to improve their delivery performance and market share.

To be successful in Europe, exporters should aim at offering the same level of delivery service and reliability in a Continental market as would a local supplier based in the country concerned. That is now quite possible through the use of international express distribution services offering overnight or 48-hour door-to-door transit for goods moving between the UK and Continental consignees.

The first point to be decided when a company is considering the use of express services is the role of distribution within its marketing strategy. Some companies, for example, currently use express delivery services purely as a back-up to handle the movement of particularly urgent consignments. Stock orders are then routed through more traditional freight transport channels.

Adopting that approach can help an exporter to avoid losing customers through failure to respond quickly to urgent situations. However, using express services on an *ad hoc* basis usually means paying higher rates. There will always be occasions when express services can fulfil a valuable 'fire brigade' role, but far greater benefits can be gained by using them as a planned, integral part of an overall distribution strategy.

In that context, it is worth noting that express services are maintained with a variety of different types of operation and transport mode. Some, for example, involve the use of aircraft to fly freight between major countries in Europe. Such operations are most often used to support overnight delivery services. Collection and delivery at either end is of course handled through the use of road vehicles.

Other operations involve the use of road vehicles for the whole transport movement. Such services sometimes offer overnight deliveries between, for example, the UK and major cities in the near Continent region but are more often used to run economy 48–72 hour services. In addition, economy services offered by express companies can normally provide faster door-to-door transit times than conventional air freight. The reason why express services are normally quicker than other methods is that they avoid port or airport bottlenecks and move goods on scheduled linehauls operating every day of the week.

The first advantage of express services is of course speed of transit. That is an important factor when a UK company, for example, wants to supply goods to one of the more distant EC markets such as southern Italy or Greece. The ability to get goods delivered to a consignee in one of those countries within, say, 48–72 hours can be a major factor in securing new business and in holding on to existing customers in increasingly competitive markets.

Coupled with speed of transport is the fact that express services normally offer published door-to-door all-inclusive rates. Also receivers can be given accurate information about when to expect shipments at their premises, so that arrangements can be made to handle consignments once they arrive on site.

Bearing these factors in mind, a company seeking an express delivery service operator should check to see whether the organisation concerned has sufficient in-house resources on the Continent to sort out quickly any problems which may occur during transit and alert customers to potential delays in delivery, so that remedial action can be taken if necessary.

The use of express distribution services should also produce some significant cash flow benefits for users. For a start, the fact that goods can be moved quickly from manufacturing point to final consignee means that stockholdings can be reduced, so saving on inventory costs. At the same time, because goods are delivered faster, the exporter will be able to demand quicker payment.

Just as important is the perceived value of receiving the goods on time. Automotive manufacturers, for example, are now very aware of the need to deliver spare parts to their dealers quickly, so the latter can in turn repair vehicles for customers as fast as possible and meet promised completion dates.

Express service operators should additionally be able to provide customers with rapid proof of delivery information, which will then in turn allow shippers to put pressure on their customers for early payment, again helping cash flow situations.

Another important advantage for users of reliable express distribution services is the flexibility they gain in terms of delivery times. Major express operators offer a choice of different service options which within Europe can range, for example, from next-morning delivery to standard next-day, 48-hour and economy (usually 72-hour) delivery services.

Exporters should look carefully at the menu of express services available and choose the most suitable options for their particular business – in many cases the best solution will involve using a mix of services. For instance, standard stock replacement consignments can be routed via an economy two-day or three-day delivery service, while more urgent items, to replace goods out of stock, or higher-value goods can be distributed by overnight delivery.

Express operators, by offering door-to-door services, can use a single consignment note for the whole transaction rather than the numerous documents required for conventional transport. In addition, express operators can handle many of the export documentation activities. And all these benefits free an exporter's staff for other work.

Selecting a specific express service operator can at first sight seem a fairly daunting task – the last few years have seen a massive expansion in the number of companies providing such services. One of the first decisions an operator has to take is whether to use just one express operator or several. The advantages of selecting a number of operators include the fact that the customer can select 'horses for courses', picking out specialists in particular markets, and can compare their delivery performances, rates, customer service, etc.

Against that, choosing to work with one particular express distribution company tends to create better opportunities for developing a genuine business partnership, with all the usual benefits which should arise from such a relationship. Operationally, for example, the express company gets the chance to develop a good understanding of the customer's overall business and, just as importantly, the business of the customer's customer, so that service performance can be better gauged to meet everyone's requirements exactly.

In recent years there have been dock strikes and customs strikes. In times such as these, companies flock to express operators, especially those with their own air linehaul network, to bypass any bottlenecks. Of course, these express operators tend to look after their existing customers first and foremost when resources are scarce.

Many of the criteria used in deciding which operator or operators to employ are the same as those which apply when choosing any third-party contractor.

- Does the company have a good record?
- Does it have a strong presence and back-up in the overseas markets concerned, and what level of control does it have over all the elements of the door-to-door transport movement?
- What level of insurance cover is provided?
- What service guarantees are offered?

- How far advanced is the service provider with the development of information technology systems which can both keep track of consignment and rapidly produce proof of delivery details and other useful management information?

A particularly important area to check out involves the arrangements for customs clearance of goods in the country of destination and the onward movement of those goods in that country to final consignee. Generally speaking, those operators with their own offices and vehicle fleets in other countries, in this case specifically those of the EC, should be better placed to exert full control over the movement of their traffic.

Assessment of any express operator has to be based first on reputation – potential new users of such services should not be afraid to ask around to check up on the experiences of other customers – and probably also on a few trial runs. Obviously the latter are not always an infallible guide – every operator has its particularly good and bad days – but such try-outs should at least give some indication of the service company's likely performance and attitude to it customers.

18. Full-load and groupage distribution

Until the comparatively recent development of intra-European express delivery services, the main freight transport options open to UK exporters trading with the Continent involved the use of either full-load or general cargo groupage operations.

Even now, those types of road-based services still account for a large proportion of the freight being moved between the UK and the Continent and look likely to continue doing so, albeit in a rather more sophisticated form which will increasingly include the use of IT systems etc.

A full-load movement is just what the name implies – an exporter with sufficient cargo to fill a vehicle or trailer either arranges such a movement in-house or contracts with a forwarder or haulier for the movement of that load to the country of destination. In some cases that involves delivering into an overseas depot where the goods are deconsolidated and then distributed to the final consignees. Where there is just one consignee, though, goods may be delivered straight through.

This sort of operation obviously has a role to play in the distribution strategy of any company which regularly generates sufficient volumes of traffic for a particular market and can justify the use of a complete vehicle or trailer. Examples might include a company exporting raw materials or components to another manufacturer.

While it should in future be easier for goods to cross borders, there are many other complications to be borne in mind in considering the possibility of operating an international haulage fleet. For a start, there is all the current uncertainty surrounding vehicle specifications – the well-publicised debate over the UK's present refusal to accept 40-tonne vehicles to bring it into line with the rest of the Community is just one example of various legislative disparities which are causing problems for vehicle fleet operators.

Then there is the problem of organising backloads to make the operation more economically viable, although with the continuing imbalance of UK/Continent traffic in favour of UK imports that might be less of a problem for companies sending goods across the Channel.

Again, though, a number of European road haulage companies have already expressed fears that liberalisation of the market will create substantial excess haulage capacity. That might mean lower rates for users of such services, but it can hardly be good news for companies operating their own vehicles and seeking backloads.

Where traffic volumes are insufficient to support full-load operations, the main alternatives are either the groupage services operated by freight forwarders and hauliers or the newer integrated service door-to-door delivery operations.

Groupage services involve the service provider, usually a freight forwarder but possibly a haulage company, receiving goods into a depot or depots from a number of customers and then consolidating their exports to particular markets into full loads. Some groupage hauliers operate regular departures, possibly daily to major destinations, while others wait until they have sufficient traffic to make up a full load.

The advantage of groupage services is that they generally offer an economic way of moving goods to the Continent, particularly if delivery time is much less important than cost. Downside factors include the less predictable transit times – smaller Continental markets may be served only once a week or even less, for instance, and even companies operating daily departures sometimes have to consolidate loads to different markets on one vehicle in order to make the operation economically viable, a move which can lead to delays.

Another potential weak link in groupage operations involves the arrangements at the receiving end. Many of the major groupage operators have either their own depots or long-established partnerships with locally based agents. In those cases, there is no real reason why groupage consignments should experience any undue delay in customs clearance and moving on to the final destination.

However, as soon as more than one party is involved in any sort of distribution operation, the potential for a breakdown in communications is that much greater. It should be noted, though, that some of the more forward-thinking groupage operators are now developing their own IT systems to reduce that risk and enable them to offer the same sort of management information feedback as is now increasingly available in other sectors of the distribution industry.

So how do you decide whether groupage services have a role to play in your particular European distribution strategy? In making that decision companies need to assess exactly who they are sending their goods to – is it, for example, an agent, distributor, end user or another part of the same organisation, that is effectively an in-house movement?

If the requirement is for the regular movement of large volumes on a factory-to-factory or factory-to-warehouse basis, the 24/48-hour transits offered by the best groupage service operators may well have a role to play, particularly if the value of the goods involved is such that they will not readily bear higher transport costs.

Such arguments are rather less convincing where goods are being delivered to an end user, a situation likely to become increasingly common as the EC barriers to trade come down.

Another subject which has to be considered in assessing the merits of groupage services involves pricing. In a typical case, the full price for an international freight movement involving the use of a road-based groupage service will involve a mixture of freight rates generally charged on a per freight tonne basis plus charges for various documentation procedures, principally relating to customs clearance operations.

In the majority of cases, however, that will not be the total transport cost of the goods. For example, on arrival at the destination depot where the cargo is to be discharged, further handling and storage charges are likely to be incurred either by the exporter or, depending on the terms of the orginal export sale, the importer.

Some people claim that this situation puts groupage services at a strong disadvantage compared with express door-to-door delivery operations which offer all-inclusive rates. However, it should also be pointed out that some organisations prefer to see exactly how their transport costs are broken down, in which case the claimed disadvantage of groupage service pricing methods is actually an advantage. Some door-to-door express operators will provide transport costs in broken-down form and of course broken shipping terms. As with most aspects of distribution strategy, there is no definite right way or wrong way. The individual company must make its own evaluation and decide which options best suit particular needs.

For companies opting to use groupage services, the final decision of course is to select an operator or operators. Again, a choice needs to be made between a groupage operator which meets all requirements and a specialist in a particular market.

The advantages of the former include the chance to build up a good partnership arrangement and simpler accounting procedures. Against that, few groupage operators cover all European markets with the same degree of frequency, so it is important to check that the service level you require is available to all the markets you want to reach.

Selecting different operators for individual export markets in Europe should help to ensure you get the best possible service frequency to each point. However, if you are shipping only a small percentage of your traffic with any one operator you are probably less well placed to build up a good relationship with the carrier, negotiate advantageous freight rates and put the pressure on if service levels start to slip.

One final point – always check out exactly what service a particular groupage operator is providing and how guaranteed the departure frequencies are. An advertised claim of '48 hours to northern Italy', for example, may look good, but the advantages to the shipper are somewhat reduced if the service is being run once a month.

19. International mail distribution

Foreign trade activities generate substantial quantities of correspondence, documents and printed matter. Exporters developing an international distribution strategy should consider the different methods of handling overseas mail. Until recently, companies organising the international distribution of mail had to use the Post Office system. The only real alternative was to send items via courier, a not particularly cost-effective option for normal correspondence or direct mail material.

Over the last few years, though, private-sector alternatives to the Post Office have begun to emerge. Such companies are now providing a growing range of services for the international distribution of business mail.

Post Office international mail services first began to develop during the mid-nineteenth century. Initially, the handling of such mail was covered by bilateral arrangements between the countries concerned. In 1862, though, the major post offices agreed to a set of common operating principles, following that up twelve years later by signing a more detailed agreement which effectively established one postal union.

That development marked the birth of the organisation which today co-ordinates international post office activities around the world, the Universal Postal Union. Through the UPU, post offices agree the charges they make on each other, with the result that such charges tend to be based more on administrative considerations than real cost. That co-operation currently rules out competition between different postal authorities.

However, the whole subject of postal services in Europe is now under review by the European Commission. At the time of writing, a long-awaited EC Green Paper detailing proposals for the future deregulation of such services is still to be published. Observers believe the Green Paper will suggest that certain key services continue to be reserved for the post offices, but that other areas of activity should be opened up to greater private sector competition.

Main international mail services now provided by the UK Post Office include:

- First-class mail, which offers the fastest non-courier delivery, often using air links, for items which can be classed as 'letters', such as business correspondence and invoices
- Printed-matter services, which offer slower but cheaper delivery for direct mail shots, brochures, magazines, etc.
- Parcel-post services, offering dependable if sometimes slow delivery of both dutiable and non-dutiable packages of normally up to around 30 kilos
- Registered mail, where proof of delivery (POD) can be provided to give added security, although confirming the POD can take several weeks depending on the destination of the mail

Several years ago, the UK Post Office decided to strengthen its service portfolio with the introduction of a product called Airstream to cater for the bulk mailing of international business mail. Subsequently, a sister product called Airstream Print was launched to cater for the mailing of printed items such as brochures and magazines.

The idea of both new services was to offer regular shippers of large volumes of traffic some substantial savings on ordinary airmail rates – rates are based on a price per kilo. In addition, such services are said to offer businesses considerable savings on their own post-room time and costs by eliminating the need to weigh and price every item of mail. Instead, the customers are provided with special Airstream sacks which enable them to bag up overseas traffic, which is then collected by the Post Office.

One of the initial drawbacks for potential users of Airstream, though, was that it was really geared only to handling business from large organisations with single postings of more than 2 kilos of international mail traffic. In a bid to make the service more accessible to smaller users, the Post Office subsequently tried linking up with selected private-sector operators, which could effectively also market the service by acting as collectors and consolidators.

Overall, Airstream is seen as the Post Office response to what has now become a major challenge for business mail traffic from private-sector operators.

The private-sector companies fall into two categories – single-point remailers and multi-point remailers. Both offer similar advantages to the Post Office Airstream operation – lower rates, reduction of post-room administration costs, etc. However, operational systems of the single-point and multi-point operators vary quite considerably.

Most remail companies operating in the UK are single-point or two-centre operators. They collect mail from their customers, sort, frank and consolidate traffic for different markets and then arrange transportation by road or air to a centre such as Brussels or Copenhagen, where the letters are handed over to another organisation, usually the local postal authority, which then arranges the onward movement to the final market. Such services can offer cost savings over standard Post Office airmail of up to 30 or 40 per cent, although delivery times will probably not be any faster.

Multi-centre remailers keep their traffic under in-house control for a much greater part of the distribution chain. They too collect, sort and consolidate traffic for their customers but then arrange the onward movement of the letters to one of their own overseas centres. Final delivery is made by hand in most of the main centres around the world or put into the local postal service. Cost savings may not be quite as marked as those achieved by using some of the cheaper single-point remailers, but they still offer considerable savings over Post Office airmail services. More importantly they provide quicker delivery times and better service.

The first decision, then, in working out the mail aspect of an international distribution strategy is whether to stick with the Post Office or choose a private remail company.

The increasingly close co-operation between postal authorities may mean that international service levels might improve over the next few years, while the more commercial approach now being adopted by the UK Post Office and its counterparts overseas could further help companies looking to negotiate contracts for their business mail traffic.

Downside factors for the UK Post Office include its vulnerability to disruptive industrial action, as illustrated towards the end of 1987 and in September 1988, a certain lack of service flexibility, which means that it would be difficult, for example, to re-route traffic via other countries in the event of problems in the UK; the fact that international mail is usually collected at the same time as domestic items, which can lead to delays in initial sorting; and the fact that once mail leaves the UK it is out of the local Post Office's control and totally in the hands of the receiving authority. The UK Post Office is generally acknowledged to be efficient by world standards in its own operations, but postal authority standards and performance vary considerably from one part of the world to another.

Private-sector operators offer the advantage of lower costs than Post Office airmail services. They also tend to be more flexible both in collection times and in their ability to re-route traffic to avoid trouble-spots. Depending on the operational system they employ, some also keep control of their traffic in-house until much further along the delivery chain, so improving service levels. Similarly, the leading private-sector operators are often able to return undelivered items more quickly than the Post Offices, which send some undelivered mail by sea rather than by air.

Another important factor which should be borne in mind, especially by companies generating large volumes of mail, is the fact that private-sector companies invoice their customers after collection, whereas payment has to be made immediately when using normal Post Office airmail services. That can have an important bearing on cash flow.

The disadvantages of using private-sector remail services include the often widely varying levels of service provided. It is important that companies considering mail options as part of an overall distribution strategy decide whether cost of service or speed and reliability are their priorities – with remail, as with many other services, you generally end up getting what you pay for. In that context, it is well worth while undertaking a few anonymous trial runs before signing any contracts. Most remailers also lack the breadth of services which can be offered by the Post Office, concentrating mainly on providing a first-class airmail service and maybe a second-tier service for printed matter.

So what questions should you ask when assessing the merits of particular remail companies?

- Firstly, what sort of operational systems does the remailer use and at what point does the company hand over control to another party? Where three or four organisations are involved in the distribution chain the potential for delays is that much greater.
- How flexible is the remailer as regards collections – can they respond, for example, to urgent or late requests for collection?
- What range of services is available to meet what might be a variety of customer needs? Generally speaking, there are more advantages to be gained, both in terms of in-house administration considerations and cost, from working with one company to handle all, or nearly all, international mail requirements than from working with a number of operators.
- What credit terms are available? The terms of payment vary quite considerably from one remail service operator to another and can become an important factor for companies looking to keep a tight hold on their cash flow situation.
- What system does the remailer employ for returning undelivered items? Some operators are normally able to get such returns back to the sender within one to three weeks, so that mailing lists can be updated and missing business contacts chased up.
- Does the remailer own its own linehaul system throughout Europe?

20. Courier distribution

Another important aspect of international trading activities which should be reviewed as part of any distribution strategy concerns the ability to move urgently needed paperwork and documents rapidly, either to and from suppliers and customers or in-house between different offices in the same organisation. Closely linked to that requirement is the need to develop a plan for handling the often equally urgent movement of small quantities of samples or spare parts to company personnel or customers in overseas markets. In fact so strong is the need for such services that a whole industry has developed over the last couple of decades specifically to handle that business.

International courier services offering fast door-to-door or desk-to-desk movement of documents and other urgently needed smaller items first came to prominence during the 1970s as the developed areas of the world, notably Europe, North America and the Far East, increasingly began to trade with emerging markets in regions such as the Middle East, Africa and Latin America.

In many cases, traditional methods of sending urgent items, for instance by post, proved unreliable for countries where transport and communication systems were often in their infancy. With exporters and traders desperate to find reliable ways of moving documents, samples and spare parts quickly from one part of the world to another, private companies moved in to fill the gaps left by international postal systems. Those new courier organisations developed their own international networks of offices to facilitate controlled desk-to-desk deliveries using the fastest mode of transport available – usually air – and their own staff or agents at all stages in the movement from collection to final delivery.

In recent years, postal authorities around the world have also developed large-scale courier operations – the UK Post Office, for example, runs both international and domestic courier services under the product name Datapost.

How do you select a courier service operator which can be relied upon to provide a service which could literally mean the difference between winning and losing important export sales orders? What questions should you ask?

- Firstly, what is the extent of the courier company's international coverage? Does it, for example, cover the whole of each country it claims to serve or merely the major centres? How much of the operation is handled in-house, where full control can be exerted, and how much involves the use of agents, particularly at the delivery end? It should be noted that many courier companies offering international services in fact simply undertake the collection of items in the UK and then consolidate traffic for onward movement via wholesaler courier linehaul operators to destination markets, at which point an agent takes over to effect customs clearance and final delivery. Such arrangements may work perfectly well, but whenever consignments leave the direct control of the principal, the potential for problems or communication breakdown is that little bit greater.
- In that context, what systems, if any, does the courier company have for tracking consignments and producing a proof of delivery quickly if requested?
- How reliable is the courier when delivering inbound packages? If, for example, you find that inbound material tends to be delivered to you early in the morning, the chances are that similar delivery times will be maintained in overseas countries, certainly in Europe.
- What sort of response do you get to requests for collection? Does the person receiving the telephone call appear to understand what you are talking about and be keen to help? Does the motorcycle rider or van driver undertaking the collection turn up when expected and appear to be both helpful and reliable? While appearances can sometimes be deceptive, a sloppy or unhelpful attitude from a telephone receptionist or pick-up driver often reflects a generally unprofessional approach by the courier company as a whole.
- How flexible is the courier company – can it respond properly to urgent one-off requests which cannot be met using its scheduled or standard services? Most leading international courier services operate to regular timetables, usually daily, to fit in with airline flight schedules. However, some courier organisations operating their own aircraft will also provide special immediate-response courier services offering the fastest possible delivery at that time. Such services are obviously fairly expensive, but the return can be worthwhile if the fast delivery of samples or documents can clinch an order worth perhaps several hundred thousand pounds.

Still on the subject of service performance and reliability, a number of the leading courier organisations offer as a regular product what is termed 'on-board courier' services, particularly to major markets generating high volumes of traffic. The courier flies on the same aircraft as the consignments. While the bags containing the consignments go in the aircraft hold, the courier keeps the accompanying paperwork in hand baggage. At the destination end, the courier hands over the paperwork either to another member of the same company or an agent, who is then responsible for getting the consignments cleared and moved on to the consignee. Major advantages of that sort of operation are speed of clearance and close control.

Having initially made their reputation as carriers of urgently needed documents and small items such as samples, most of these international courier companies are now rapidly broadening the scope of their operations to take in other areas of business. Many courier organisations, for example, now offer services catering for parcels larger than the 30-kilo limit normally applied to international air courier bags. Increasingly, operators talk about their 'air express' rather than 'courier' services to get over the message that they are now handling the worldwide distribution of parcels, general freight and bulk mail as well as more traditional document-type traffic.

However, potential customers should be careful to check that courier companies claiming to cater for larger traffic as well as document-type items actually have the systems to handle it properly. Within Europe, for example, many courier companies often use quite small light aircraft to move their traffic overnight, which means that they would struggle to cope with many larger items. Better to check beforehand that the chosen courier would, for example, be able to handle ten 50-kilo parcels at short notice than find out the next morning that they were not shipped as planned because there was no room on the aircraft!

Another courier industry development of potential interest to UK companies seeking to develop their export business involves the move by some organisations to introduce their own electronic data transmission services. Basically, those operators combine the use of facsimile-style equipment with their extensive office/agent networks to meet the needs of customer companies which either do not have electronic data transmission equipment of their own or are working with other organisations which do not.

The UK Post Office, for instance, has over the last few years established a firm presence in the field of document transmission through a public facsimile service called Intelpost. Users have the option of either linking into the Intelpost system electronically by using compatible fax equipment, telex or computer, or handing in material at designated Intelpost Post Offices for transmission to UK or overseas destinations, where documents can be picked up during normal hours or delivered by messenger.

V

Transport in the member states

Introduction

European managers face a complicated network of transport services in each market. The transport heritage of each member state within the EC is closely related to other physical and cultural factors. Environmental and economic constraints have been met by technological progress and industrial pressures to provide an uneven maze of transport across the EC.

Even after 1992, transport and traffic policies will continue to be set at national level, although a greater number of decisions will be taken at the Community level. As has been the case throughout history, industry will develop distribution systems around the advantages of transport networks. Distribution systems which are designed to meet the needs of industry are emerging across Europe and providers of transport services are becoming more aware of and more capable of meeting the particular needs of their clients.

International trade and transport is continuing its thirty-year growth pattern. Deregulation and privatisation are removing barriers of bureaucracy and ideology, letting the private sector address the demands of the global market place for a gradual increase in the flow of trade at faster and better costs.

Although service providers are considering the needs of the client more carefully, it remains the responsibility of the transport user to determine the best means of transporting components to the factory and goods to the market place. Europe is and will remain a patchwork of customs, languages, labour situations and taxation.

Companies which are familiar with the characteristics of transport systems in each market in which they do business will be more able to recognise and implement sound systems to meet their particular needs. In this section we examine the characteristics of each transport market by mode to give some knowledge of each market in the EC.

Benelux

In 1944 the Netherlands formed the Benelux Economic Union with Belgium and Luxembourg. The main goal was to abolish import duties within the three countries and to establish common tariffs for imports from outside Benelux. The Treaty of Rome, 1957, formed the EC, which minimised the latter's importance. However, Benelux is still used as a yardstick for new policies of the EC. Because of the position of the Benelux members on tariffs, the transport system of the three members has become integrated to a degree higher than in other Continental markets. Each country, however, maintains its own internal regulations and systems and each has developed unique characteristics, which are mainly related to topography and trading heritage.

Belgium

Belgium boasts one of the best road networks in the world, with over 45 kilometres of motorway per square kilometre of land mass. The road network links the important ports of Antwerp and Rotterdam in the Netherlands to southern and eastern markets of France and West Germany and the UK market across the Channel. Belgium handles a disproportionately large percentage of Europe's goods. Internal connections in the Belgian market are very good. Major proposed changes to the Belgian transport network are an extension of the French high-speed train services to Brussels and perhaps onwards and various proposals for reducing the public-sector payments for the road network. Belgium's main airport, Brussels Zaventem, provides international service competition to Amsterdam. Domestic air transport of goods is very limited.

In 1985 the total quantity of goods transported by national transport organisations in Belgium was over 466 million tonnes. Figure 15 shows the breakdown by mode.

Figure 15: Total quantity of goods transported by national transport organisations in Belgium in 1985 by mode

Mode of transport	Million tonnes	Percentage
Rail	72.4	15.52
Road	300.8	64.49
Inland waterways	93.2	19.98
Total	466.4	100

Figure 16: Total traffic by group of goods and mode of transport in Belgium

	Road	Rail	Inland waterways	Total
Cereals	3,729	1,659	6,211	11,599
Potatoes, fresh/frozen fruit, vegetables	6,756	170	32	6,958
Live animals, sugar beet	6,143	139	–	6,282
Wood, cork	6,447	346	221	7,014
Textiles, man-made fibres	3,170	41	22	3,233
Foodstuffs, animal fodder	41,234	1,457	4,419	47,110
Oil seeds, oleaginous fruits/fats	1,122	264	1,804	3,190
Solid mineral fuels	9,484	13,885	5,348	28,717
Crude petroleum	25	–	435	460
Petroleum products	12,892	3,070	21,845	37,807
Iron ore, iron and steel waste	3,206	15,933	3,465	22,604
Non-ferrous ores and waste	120	617	1,604	2,341
Metal products	11,710	16,344	7,944	35,998
Cement, lime, building material	30,289	1,130	1,993	33,412
Crude and manufactured minerals	97,517	2,420	23,430	123,367
Natural and chemical fertilisers	9,220	1,297	5,237	15,754
Coals, chemicals, tar	283	32	364	679
Other chemicals	12,679	2,630	6,824	22,133
Paper pulp, waste paper	1,044	1,520	497	3,061
Transport equipment, machinery	7,366	30	1,888	9,284
Manufactures of metal	4,921	243	62	5,226
Glass, glassware, ceramic products	3,682	138	15	3,835
Leather, textile, clothing	10,474	6,252	76	16,802
Miscellaneous articles	14,364	66,802	968	82,134
Total	297,877	136,419	94,704	529,000

Road

Carriage of freight by road is the most important transport mode in Belgium. This is due to the central government's commitment to building the best motorway network in Europe in the early 1970s. This is a clear case of infrastructure development influencing transport users' development.

Unlike those in the Netherlands, Belgian companies tend to prefer to ship on their own account. There is a gradual trend towards contracting out for transport services, and there is evidence to suggest that this will be a growing trend as service providers become more competitive and develop specialised services.

Over 45 per cent of the international road freight which is loaded in Belgium is destined for France, West Germany and the Netherlands. Belgium's geographical position between the major trading countries and the development of Antwerp as one of Europe's leading ports have led to the country becoming the crossroads of Europe.

Rail

The major north–south link for freight on the Belgian rail system has maintained its usefulness, and it is interesting to note that over 55 per cent of the total revenue realised by the rail network is generated by freight.

Although the Belgian government has favoured the development of the road network in recent years, the success of the French TGV network generated renewed interest in railway development. The Belgian government is currently examining an extension of the high-speed rail network to Brussels and on to West Germany. However, the third stage of the plan would have only limited capacity for freight.

Long-distance carriage of coal, ore and steel was the main reason for the development of the Belgian rail system. In recent years the rail system has developed to serve the grain and food-related industries of the northern region and the chemical industry, which is strongly linked to the West German, Dutch and UK markets.

Inland waterways

The canal system which links the port region in and around Antwerp to the manufacturers and distributors in and near Brussels is quite important. Connections from the canal system to road and rail are very good. Several canal links provide international services between the port area and the Limburg region of the Netherlands and to the northern provinces of France through Flanders. The canal connections are growing in popularity for transport of agricultural products.

Air

Freight-handling facilities at Brussels' Zaventem and Antwerp's Diegem airports are geared towards international transit. The development of the express freight industry at Zaventem and the intermodal aspects developed around the seaport of Antwerp have created a flexible and efficient transport services infrastructure. Most major carriers serve Zaventem. New combined services provided by international carriers mean that passenger service schedules supplement the international cargo flight schedules.

To show the development of the air freight market the figures below give the tonnage of freight carried by the national flag carrier, Sabena, from 1984 to 1987.

Year	Tonnes carried (000s)
1984	79.8
1985	87.7
1986	87.6
1987	90.9

Express services

Air express companies have recognised the central position of Zaventem and have developed sorting hubs and overland delivery networks to meet the needs of this region. Connections to Paris, London, the Netherlands and West Germany are best. New services have improved service levels to North America and the Asian Pacific markets. Because the express service industry entered Belgium in the early days of the growth of the industry, major improvements will be not in facilities expansion but in applications of IT. Belgium's telecommunication network regulation provides for the independent development of private, closed networks.

The growth of the express service sector in Belgium can be demonstrated by the number of shipments being dispatched by this method. In 1981 some 0.1 million were moved. By 1983 this had grown to 0.3 million shipments and by 1987 to 1.2 million shipments. This type of growth is typical of other countries.

Combined transport

The local combined transport organisation, TRW, showed the following development in units dispatched during the years 1983–6.

Year	Number of units
1983	13.075
1984	13.810
1985	15.161
1986	17.193

Percentage change 1985–6 = 13.4%

Luxembourg

Luxembourg's small size and strategic position have fostered the development of through ways of transport. The river, road and rail networks in Luxembourg serve the neighbouring industries in France, West Germany and Belgium. Internal transport is mainly by road, although agriculture and some heavy industry take advantage of the strong rail and river facilities.

In 1985 the total quantity of goods transported by national transport organisations in Luxembourg was over 43 million tonnes. Figure 17 shows the breakdown by mode.

Figure 17: Total quantity of goods transported by national transport organisations in Luxembourg in 1985 by mode

Mode of transport	Million tonnes	Percentage
Rail	17.6	40.84
Road	15.8	36.66
Inland waterways	9.7	22.50
Total	43.1	100

Figure 18: Total traffic by group of goods and mode of transport in Luxembourg				
	Road	Rail	Inland waterways	Total
Cereals	13	70	1,383	1,466
Potatoes, fresh/frozen fruit, vegetables	125	51	–	176
Live animals, sugar beet	22	–	–	22
Wood, cork	164	39	2	205
Textiles, man-made fibres	8	28	–	36
Foodstuffs, animal fodder	1,118	3	138	1,259
Oil seeds, oleaginous fruits/fats	–	–	184	184
Solid mineral fuels	137	2,301	1,820	4,258
Crude petroleum	–	606	–	606
Petroleum products	1,077	1,295	682	3,054
Iron ore, iron and steel waste	477	2,843	1,758	5,078
Non-ferrous ores and waste	75	12	27	114
Metal products	717	4,474	1,046	6,237
Cement, lime, building material	877	346	303	1,526
Crude and manufactured minerals	7,823	82	1,909	9,814
Natural and chemical fertilisers	245	509	191	945
Coals, chemicals, tar	6	3	–	9
Other chemicals	269	178	54	501
Paper pulp, waste paper	–	1	–	1
Transport equipment, machinery	284	88	3	375
Manufactures of metal	138	6	6	150
Glass, glassware, ceramic products	331	31	–	362
Leather, textile, clothing	184	23	–	207
Miscellaneous articles	237	2,122	–	2,359
Total	14,327	15,111	9,506	38,944

Road

Luxembourg has not developed an extensive road network like its Benelux partners, though through transport via road is good. The main reason has been the lack of domestic need, the agricultural economic base being sufficiently served by existing roadways. Luxembourg now has 16 kilometres of motorway per square kilometre of land mass, which is an eight-fold increase since 1970.

In 1985 Luxembourg hauliers moved nearly 16 million tonnes of goods by road. This accounted for 36.7 per cent of the total moved, and it is interesting to note that Luxembourg is one of the few countries where a higher tonnage of goods is moved by rail than road.

Rail

The total traffic moved by rail in 1985 was nearly 18 million tonnes and accounts for the greatest proportion of freight moved. The predominant users of the rail system are the coal and steel producers based in Luxembourg.

Inland waterways

National transport operators moved some 9.7 million tonnes of goods via the inland waterway system in 1986. The predominant use of the Luxembourg canal system, though, is to service the major heavy industries of its neighbours in West Germany, France and Belgium.

Air

Air connections with Luxembourg city airport are not as good as those with Amsterdam and Brussels. However, freight-handling facilities are good and international air freight movement in Luxembourg is expected to increase in the coming years, although from a very small base. Only 9,000 tonnes of freight were forwarded on passenger services in 1987 from Luxembourg.

Express services

Express services are not well developed in Luxembourg mainly because there is little manufacturing capacity to support the industry. However, the banking and financial sectors do provide a limited amount of traffic. In 1987, 200,000 shipments were despatched via express services.

The Netherlands

The Netherlands has developed a highly efficient road transport sector. Freight transport by rail has been limited to local delivery in the Rotterdam port area, although rail may become more important for the domestic transport of goods as the major trunkroads reach peak-hour capacities. The inland waterway system is the most developed and efficient in the world and is used by most industry sectors. In 1985 the total quantity of goods transported by national transport organisations in the Netherlands was 665.1 million tonnes. Figure 19 shows the breakdown by mode.

Figure 19: Total quantity of goods transported by national transport organisations in the Netherlands in 1985 by mode

Mode of transport	Million tonnes	Percentage
Rail	20.2	3.04
Road	390.8	58.76
Inland waterways	254.1	38.20
Total	665.1	100

Road

The road network in the Netherlands is second only to Belgium in terms of density, with over 43 kilometres per square kilometre of land mass. The Netherlands has a highly developed national and international road distribution industry and is considered to be the leading country in Europe for international road haulage companies.

In 1985 Dutch hauliers moved over 390 million tonnes of goods by road. This figure is made up of international traffic of over 50 million tonnes and domestic traffic of 340 million tonnes. An interesting point is that in the domestic sector only 34.7 per cent of traffic in tonnes was handled by own-account operators, showing a highly developed hire and reward sector. This trend is also seen in the international sector, with only approximately 10 per cent of traffic in tonnes being handled by own-account operators.

Rail

The total traffic moved by rail amounted to over 20 million tonnes in 1985. In this sector international transport accounted for over 14 million tonnes, or 72.4 per cent, compared to 5.5 million tonnes for national transport. These figures reflect the long-haul competitiveness of rail transport. Although some growth can be expected in the rail market in the Netherlands, there is little doubt that road is the dominant mover of goods.

Figure 20: Total traffic by group of goods and mode of transport in the Netherlands

	Road	Rail	Inland waterways	Total
Cereals	2,023	237	7,536	9,796
Potatoes, fresh/frozen fruit, vegetables	16,983	158	663	17,804
Live animals, sugar beet	11,889	322	9	12,220
Wood, cork	6,627	36	467	7,130
Textiles, man-made fibres	4,338	40	100	4,478
Foodstuffs, animal fodder	83,117	670	17,406	101,193
Oil seeds, oleaginous fruits/fats	2,647	59	5,530	8,236
Solid mineral fuels	1,339	1,112	17,600	20,051
Crude petroleum	11	855	2,004	2,870
Petroleum products	16,850	570	41,046	58,466
Iron ore, iron and steel waste	2,212	3,205	34,534	39,951
Non-ferrous ores and waste	499	52	3,123	3,674
Metal products	9,629	842	10,131	20,602
Cement, lime, building material	26,350	350	3,487	30,187
Crude and manufactured minerals	99,884	1,991	84,288	186,163
Natural and chemical fertilisers	6,175	1,551	8,761	16,487
Coals, chemicals, tar	249	20	591	860
Other chemicals	30,090	3,225	23,929	57,244
Paper pulp, waste paper	2,340	53	1,382	3,775
Transport equipment, machinery	8,904	273	476	9,653
Manufactures of metal	3,516	14	1,878	5,408
Glass, glassware, ceramic products	2,777	36	47	2,860
Leather, textile, clothing	17,291	133	245	17,669
Miscellaneous articles	34,629	4,467	5,363	44,459
Total	390,369	20,271	270,596	681,236

Inland waterways

The canal networks in the Netherlands have been used for centuries to transport goods from the ports to the local factories and merchants, while the agricultural sector has used waterways to send crops to world markets. Although the canals in the interior of the cities are used less today than before for local deliveries, the waterways are still a vital part of the transport system. The main arteries carry goods to and from ports to the Rhine river and onwards to Germany, Switzerland and France. Secondary systems provide an internal network covering the whole of the domestic market.

The quantity of goods transported by inland waterways in the Netherlands is growing. From 1985 to 1986 there was a growth of 6.5 per cent in total tonnage moved, from 254 million tonnes to over 270 million tonnes. In the inland water sector national transport accounted for some 155.5 million tonnes, with international transport accounting for some 82.6 million tonnes. It is interesting to note that more tonnage is moved internationally by inland water than by both road and rail systems put together.

Air

Air transport of goods within the Netherlands is limited because of the small size of the home market. However, connections are good and local airports with freight-handling facilities are numerous. The northern province of Groningen and the southern province of Limburg each have strong links with the flagship airport at Amsterdam's Schipol. However, the main use of air freight is for external trade. Together with the seaport of Rotterdam, Schipol airport handles over 40 per cent of all goods transported within the EC and most of the major airlines of the world connect with Schipol airport. Highly sophisticated freight-handling facilities have been built and further facilities are under development.

To show the development of the air freight market, the figures below show the tonnage of freight carried by the national flag carrier KLM from 1984 to 1987.

Year	Tonnes carried (000s)
1984	218.1
1985	214.5
1986	232.0
1987	267.9

Express services

Because of the central position of the Netherlands to the markets of the UK, West Germany, France and Belgium, the major express operators have established sorting hubs and networks here. Amsterdam's Schipol airport and Maastricht's Beek airport are central to the European operations of many of the major service providers. The Dutch government has supported the growth of the express industry in the Netherlands by taking a liberal political attitude towards postal deliveries, and competitive rates and delivery schedules have resulted.

The growth of the express service sector can be demonstrated by the number of shipments being dispatched by this method. In 1981, some 0.1 million shipments were moved. By 1983 this had grown to 0.3 million and by 1987 to 1.6 million shipments. This trend reflects the more recent developments in the express market and the growing acceptance by transport users of the associated benefits.

Combined transport

The drive to provide seamless services for transport is leading major providers to develop combined transport services and related services such as warehousing and depot services. The port of Rotterdam has led the way in privatising many aspects of its operations in order to accelerate the expansion of combined transport services. The concept of road/rail combined transport has not yet gained the level of acceptance in the Netherlands that it has in other countries, but it is growing, and the opening of the new terminal at Ede will assist.

The local combined transport organisation, Trailstar, showed the following development in units dispatched during the years 1983–6.

Year	Number of units
1983	5,445
1984	4,887
1985	5,588
1986	6,187

Percentage change 1985–6 = 10.7%

Summary

The Benelux market is very well served by all modes of transport. The central governments of each of the three countries have put transport as a top priority for future development. The internal networks serve international markets and, therefore, inland and outward connections and support services are exceptionally strong. The traditions of international trade in these markets predispose them to serving foreign companies.

Denmark

This country lies in a strategic position between Scandinavia and West Germany and the trading region of the North Sea. As a result of its location, the sea, rail and road links are vital. Strong central planning has enabled Denmark to develop an aggressive transport industry.

In 1985 the total quantity of goods transported by national transport organisations in Denmark was over 215 million tonnes. Figure 21 shows the breakdown by transport mode.

Figure 21: Total quantity of goods transported by national transport organisations in Denmark in 1985 by mode

Mode of transport	Million tonnes	Percentage
Rail	6.7	3.11
Road	208.5	96.89
Inland waterways	n/a	—
Total	215.2	100

Road

Denmark's limited motorway system provides north-to-south connections from Sweden to the Netherlands. This 400-kilometre connection is an important link for large Swedish manufacturing companies and Danish agricultural and fisheries industries.

Rail

Denmark's rail system handles little freight overall. However, a very efficient service has been developed on the north-to-south axis to provide excellent communication between Scandinavia and the West German markets. It is significant that the two major European railway plans under consideration at the European Commission exclude Denmark, with northern termini at Hamburg and Amsterdam.

Figure 22: Total traffic by group of goods and mode of transport in Denmark

	Road	Rail	Inland waterways	Total
Cereals	7,330	5	–	7,335
Potatoes, fresh/frozen fruit, vegetables	2,281	91	–	2,372
Live animals, sugar beet	3,679	–	–	3,679
Wood, cork	7,552	553	–	8,105
Textiles, man-made fibres	416	29	–	445
Foodstuffs, animal fodder	41,999	495	–	42,494
Oil seeds, oleaginous fruits/fats	815	5	–	820
Solid mineral fuels	1,537	35	–	1,572
Crude petroleum	466	–	–	466
Petroleum products	12,106	26	–	12,132
Iron ore, iron and steel waste	1,545	56	–	1,601
Non-ferrous ores and waste	267	17	–	284
Metal products	3,316	741	–	4,057
Cement, lime, building material	16,759	73	–	16,832
Crude and manufactured minerals	61,366	182	–	61,518
Natural and chemical fertilisers	4,853	336	–	5,189
Coals, chemicals, tar	5,820	12	–	5,832
Other chemicals	2,799	347	–	3,146
Paper pulp and waste paper	1,178	161	–	1,339
Transport equipment, machinery	3,854	375	–	4,229
Manufactures of metal	1,974	28	–	2,002
Glass, glassware, ceramic products	922	75	–	997
Leather, textile, clothing	4,888	509	–	5,397
Miscellaneous articles	20,758	249	–	21,007
Total	208,450	4,400	–	212,850

Air

Denmark has international freight air links to all major European trading centres. A national priority has been set to push for the further liberalisation of the airline industry and to develop strong bilateral agreements in order to strengthen the freight transport sector in Denmark.

To show the development of the air freight sector the following figures show the tonnage of freight carried by SAS from 1984 to 1987.

Year	Tonnes carried 000s
1984	90.6
1985	91.7
1986	93.2
1987	94.8

Express services

Denmark has a relatively highly developed express industry for international connections. Internal express is important because of the fragmented nature of the market in population and geographic mass terms. The forecast for growth of express services is strong owing to the high-quality links with non-EC country markets.

Combined transport

Combined transport is not highly developed in Denmark, although there are now twelve interchange points for road/rail transit. All these points have facilities for swap bodies and containers and the majority have trailer facilities.

Summary

Denmark's economy is largely dependent upon its inland road network. Rail links serve the country, but are best for north and south links. International air connections are strong and important, especially as Eastern European markets become more important.

France

Road transport is the dominant mode for surface transportation. France has invested in transport infrastructure to meet the needs of the future through intermodal transport services. Investment in rail and water transport parallels the growth in overall transport volume. The private sector has had a major role recently in the development of trunk roads, bridges and rail networks.

There are an estimated 28,900 companies (1985) in the road transport sector. It is estimated that about 200 companies offer comprehensive distribution services and these companies account for about 15 per cent of the turnover of the industry.

In 1985 the total quantity of goods transported by national transport organisations in France was over 1,455 million tonnes. Figure 23 shows the breakdown by mode.

Figure 23: Total quantity of goods transported by national transport organisations in France in 1985 by mode

Mode of transport	Million tonnes	Percentage
Rail	158.3	10.88
Road	1,232.7	84.72
Inland waterways	64.1	4.40
Total	1,455.1	100

Road

The French motorway network has been developed through a co-operation of the public and private sectors. This has led to user fees in the form of tolls on the major motorways which have been built since the mid-1970s. Over 20 per cent of the total road traffic of the EC travels over French motorways.

Figure 24: Total traffic by group of goods and mode of transport in France

	Road	Rail	Inland waterways	Total
Cereals	47,263	11,480	7,892	66,635
Potatoes, fresh/frozen fruit, vegetables	18,753	2,076	39	20,868
Live animals, sugar beet	30,998	141	–	31,139
Wood, cork	26,326	1,459	73	27,858
Textiles, man-made fibres	10,194	187	8	10,389
Foodstuffs, animal fodder	156,114	11,672	1,591	169,377
Oil seeds, oleaginous fruits/fats	5,510	1,268	886	7,664
Solid mineral fuels	14,521	17,505	4,618	36,644
Crude petroleum	256	362	101	719
Petroleum products	63,511	12,846	9,634	85,991
Iron ore, iron and steel waste	11,073	11,585	1,769	24,427
Non-ferrous ores and waste	11,102	1,958	678	13,738
Metal products	23,743	25,247	2,754	51,744
Cement, lime, building material	99,938	3,656	178	103,772
Crude and manufactured minerals	514,565	16,136	29,532	560,233
Natural and chemical fertilisers	32,132	6,742	1,638	40,512
Coals, chemicals, tar	166	428	176	770
Other chemicals	25,913	9,692	752	36,357
Paper pulp, waste paper	3,650	918	411	4,979
Transport equipment, machinery	25,168	4,061	240	29,469
Manufactures of metal	8,193	475	38	8,706
Glass, glassware, ceramic products	7,010	1,061	11	8,082
Leather, textile, clothing	32,927	1,864	50	34,841
Miscellaneous articles	63,627	13,677	48	77,352
Total	1,232,653	156,496	63,117	1,452,266

The main destinations for goods transported by road are West Germany, the Netherlands and Belgium. Road connections to Spain and Italy are becoming increasingly important owing to the relative rise in trade coming from these two countries.

There has been a steady increase in volume of goods per kilometre transported in France over the past ten years by road. This trend is expected to continue, while the overall percentage of goods transported by truck *vis-à-vis* rail is stabilising.

There is a strong trend in the French transport services industry towards providing integrated and specialised transport services. For example, refrigerated transported services have reported a 15 per cent growth in turnover per year for the last three years.

Rail

The French railways provide a high-productivity transport system for long-haul transport. Some industrial and agricultural regions are served by local diesel-driven freight trains. The intermodal connections are not very well developed except in the case of the very large industrial companies with private sidings.

Progress in the high-speed passenger train network (TGV) has not carried over to freight services yet. It is forecast that future development should apply high-speed technology to freight services. 22-tonne axle loads could be carried at speeds of 160 to 200 kilometres per hour between major centres by the turn of the century. These speeds and load ranges will make trains quite competitive with other transport modes in the domestic French market.

Inland waterways

Inland water transport has traditionally provided links for bulk materials from the port areas to the major centres. The canal and river systems of eastern France are well connected to the West German and Benelux waterway systems, while the river Seine provides an important link between Paris and Le Havre.

Little development has taken place in the inland waterway system recently and this has resulted in lower usage. This is especially true of the major canal systems in the southern part of the country.

Air

Air Inter (Air France) together with UTA provide very good air freight services within France and between French cities and major international markets. The hub and spoke system as developed in the USA is being applied in France, with feeder flights going to hubs at Paris, Lyon and Marseille for onward connections to all parts of the globe. France has strong connections with Africa and its air system can serve these markets well.

Express services

Paris and, to a lesser extent, Lyon have played key roles in the development of the European express freight services sector.

Dedicated facilities at Paris and streamlined customs clearance provide rapid international and onward domestic handling.

To show the development of the express services sector in recent years, the number of express shipments dispatched between 1981 and 1987 is shown below.

Year	Number of shipments (millions)
1981	0.1
1983	0.5
1987	2.0

Combined transport

It is estimated that about 200 companies (1985) offer comprehensive distribution services, including combined transport facilities. The local combined transport organisation Novatrans showed the following development in units during the years 1983–6.

Year	Number of units
1983	33,556
1984	35,045
1985	39,803
1986	43,482

Percentage change 1985–6 = 9.2%

Summary

The large French market has benefited from planned and aggressive investment in the transport infrastructure. All major cities and towns are well served by road, rail and air. The inland waterways are quite limited by comparison, although some rivers meet local and long-haul transport needs. France has taken the lead in high-speed rail development and has focused on the development of the express services sector for internal and international connections.

Germany

Emerging, as it is, from the integration of the differing economies and political ideologies of East and West Germany, the new Germany faces a range of major industrial challenges and opportunities. Lack of investment in infrastructure, industry, technology and human resources over recent decades has caused severe economic problems within East Germany.

West Germany, with one of the strongest, more sophisticated industrial bases and economies in the EC, is applying the full range of its expertise and resources to the regeneration of East Germany. The extent of investment required, although not yet fully known, and the strain being imposed upon the West Germany economy are producing a range of challenges and opportunities for the whole of EEC industry. Lack of investment in infrastructure and industry meant patchy and unco-ordinated transportation and distribution systems with an acute shortage of expertise in these specialist areas. There is undoubtedly scope for the involvement of EC countries in the development of transport and distribution within East Germany.

In the absence of reliable data and known investment requirements, the statistical data of this chapter has been confined to West Germany.

The West German transport industry is well developed and considered a major industry, with over 36.5 billion DM turnover in 1986. As an important employer and source of tax revenue the industry is very closely monitored by the central government in Bonn, which has resulted in a highly regulated industry. West Germany has taken strong positions in the European Commission's discussions on the liberalisation of transport between member states. Overall internal transport is efficient and the whole system is characterised by its high level of integration of services.

In 1985 the total quantity of goods transported by national transport organisations in West Germany was over 2,806 million tonnes. Figure 31 shows the breakdown by mode.

Figure 31: Total quantity of goods transported by national transport organisations in the Republic of Ireland in 1985 by mode

Mode of transport	Million tonnes	Percentage
Rail	321.3	11.45
Road	2,262.4	80.62
Inland waterways	222.4	7.93
Total	2,806.1	100

Figure 32: Total traffic by group of goods and mode of transport in West Germany

	Road	Rail	Inland waterways	Total
Cereals	17,044	375	6,972	24,391
Potatoes, fresh/frozen fruit, vegetables	19,635	1,510	26	21,171
Live animals, sugar beet	15,510	4,347	3	19,860
Wood, cork	41,157	5,507	751	47,415
Textiles, man-made fibres	10,704	994	144	11,842
Foodstuffs, animal fodder	205,355	5,911	6,591	217,857
Oil seeds, oleaginous fruits/fats	3,907	929	5,357	10,193
Solid mineral fuels	49,272	86,615	23,823	159,710
Crude petroleum	746	1,100	117	1,963
Petroleum products	127,800	25,089	45,478	198,367
Iron ore, iron and steel waste	13,846	40,424	35,727	89,997
Non-ferrous ores and waste	2,198	1,768	3,800	7,766
Metal products	59,085	55,223	13,870	128,178
Cement, lime, building material	129,738	5,368	2,185	137,291
Crude and manufactured minerals	1,056,574	21,142	59,271	1,136,987
Natural and chemical fertilisers	8,195	10,932	6,389	25,516
Coals, chemicals, tar	2,591	1,300	1,594	5,485
Other chemicals	204,139	16,813	11,794	232,746
Paper pulp, waste paper	5,428	2,276	1,971	9,675
Transport equipment, machinery	42,203	9,252	611	52,066
Manufactures of metal	28,002	1,007	220	29,229
Glass, glassware, ceramic products	8,942	803	125	9,870
Leather, textile, clothing	73,382	4,271	443	78,096
Miscellaneous articles	137,966	17,563	2,233	157,762
Total	2,263,419	320,519	229,495	2,813,433

Road

In recent years the growth of road transport has come mainly from the international sector, which has recognised the strength of the industry's local operations. There are about 9,000 long-distance transport companies in West Germany, compared with some 32,500 companies in other sectors with their own long-distance transport capability.

Warehousing is a particularly important add-on service, with over 42 per cent of transport companies in the market offering warehousing/depot services.

West Germany's road transport industry is one of the most regulated in Europe. There are strictly enforced tariff controls imposed on pricing levels, resulting in transport rates being some 30–40 per cent higher on average than those in other member states. In order to enter the West German haulage industry, companies have to pass strict quantitative and qualitative controls which have limited capacity in the industry.

However, road transport is expected to grow in the West German market and is expected to account for 60 per cent of all transport by the year 2000, compared to 50 per cent in 1987.

Rail

The Deutsche Bundesbahn (DBB) is a very efficient system for the transport of raw and semi-finished materials for the coal, steel and related industries. The Saar and Ruhr river regions are well connected to the northern areas and especially Hamburg. The bulk chemical production in the same region benefits from the rail system and is likely to continue to support development of rail freight services.

The DBB has several feasibility studies in preparation for linking the West German rail system with the French TGV system via Cologne and Brussels. It would appear that this link will bring a much-needed improvement in long-haul international rail transport between West Germany and southern Europe.

Inland waterways

The Rhine and Ruhr rivers are the main arteries for inland transport in West Germany. These river systems provide important links for heavy industries and for the petrochemical sectors for domestic transport, as well as serving the major ports located in the Netherlands and

Belgium. The Rhine river system also acts as a link for goods moving from West Germany to France and Switzerland and as a transit link for goods moving to and from the major ports.

The future for inland water transport is positive. Intermodal services are being developed by the public and private sector and the whole system will receive an additional boost with the completion of the Rhine–Danube canal.

Air

The West German air network has been highly controlled, with Lufthansa, the national flag carrier, dominating both passenger and freight services. There are a large number of domestic airports which are well served, although at higher than average rates. The major advantage of the domestic airports is their proximity to major city centres.

Frankfurt airport has developed as a major European hub for air freight movements and has excellent links to other European and Continental centres. Cologne airport has rapidly developed as a major hub for European and worldwide express freight operators utilising their own aircraft fleets.

To show the development of the air freight market, the figures below show the tonnage of freight carried by Lufthansa from 1984 to 1987.

Year	Tonnes carried 000s
1984	308.0
1985	311.3
1986	357.4
1987	399.4

Express services

The highly regulated postal service in West Germany has inhibited the early growth of the major express services in the market. Recent moves to liberalise the postal and telecommunications sectors have supported fast growth. All major metropolitan markets are well served by express service companies.

The growth of the express services sector can be shown by the increasing number of shipments moved by this method. In 1981 some 0.1 million shipments were dispatched by express services and this had grown to some 2.5 million shipments by 1987.

Combined transport

West Germany has been one of the major proponents of combined transport and has developed the Rollende Landstrasse system for moving vehicles and trailers by rail on an international transit and domestic basis. There are some seventy-eight road/rail interchange points in West Germany. The development of the combined transport sector has in part been a response to the regulated road haulage environment.

To show the growth of combined transport the following figures show the number of units despatched by Kombiverkehr between 1983 and 1986.

Year	Number of units
1983	66,650
1984	77,600
1985	87,500
1986	106,000

Percentage change 1985–6 = 21.1%

Summary

West Germany's strong industrial base and transport infrastructure are set against a political background of heavy regulation. Transport services are of a very high quality at a very high cost. Pending liberalisation moves may result in improved flexibility and competitive pricing. All major markets are well served by advanced rail, road and air networks. The rivers provide economical transport of industrial supplies and products.

Greece

The Greek transport sector is increasingly dependent upon road transport. The value and volume of goods transported via the ports is significant but is not considered in the assessment of the inland waterways. The central government has been encouraging industry to decentralise out of the urban population centres. As a result, the importance of road links has increased.

Greek transportation legislation has recently been harmonised with the predominant EC legislation. This has required new companies to meet more stringent requirements and has resulted in an upgrading of overall service quality at both the national and international levels.

All of the main islands are connected with Athens by both ferry lines and airlines.

In 1985 the total quantity of goods transported by national transport organisations in Greece was over 163 million tonnes. Figure 25 shows the breakdown by mode.

Road

In 1989, the roadway network is still in need of considerable improvement. There are about 1,000 kilometres of national trunk road, connecting the Yugloslavian frontiers with Patia (the main western port)

Figure 25: Total quantity of goods transported by national transport organisations in Greece in 1985 by mode

Mode of transport	Million tonnes	Percentage
Rail	4.0	2.44
Road	159.7	97.56
Inland waterways	negligible	—
Total	163.7	100

Figure 26: Total traffic by group of goods and mode of transport in Greece

	Road	Rail	Inland waterways	Total
Cereals	5,520	1	–	5,521
Potatoes, fresh/frozen fruit, vegetables	3,446	177	–	3,623
Live animals, sugar beet	892	457	–	1,349
Wood, cork	3,150	82	–	3,232
Textiles, man-made fibres	706	27	–	733
Foodstuffs, animal fodder	11,354	55	–	11,409
Oil seeds, oleaginous fruits/fats	554	1	–	555
Solid mineral fuels	4,031	488	–	4,519
Crude petroleum	332	1,043	–	1,375
Petroleum products	9,683	307	–	9,990
Iron ore, iron and steel waste	207	182	–	389
Non-ferrous ores and waste	4,370	13	–	4,383
Metal products	2,791	246	–	3,037
Cement, lime, building material	29,504	12	–	29,516
Crude and manufactured minerals	53,550	66	–	53,616
Natural and chemical fertilisers	1,347	203	–	1,550
Coals, chemicals, tar	4,516	12	–	4,528
Other chemicals	2,084	132	–	2,216
Paper pulp, waste paper	407	22	–	429
Transport equipment, machinery	2,275	203	–	2,478
Manufactures of metal	973	18	–	991
Glass, glassware, ceramic products	527	16	–	543
Leather, textile, clothing	3,108	96	–	3,204
Miscellaneous articles	14,394	62	–	14,456
Total	159,721	3,921	–	163,642

through Thessaloniki and Athens. This network is currently being converted gradually into motorway, which will accelerate the development of the transport network.

Rail

The Greek railway network, compared with the northern European network, is relatively under-developed and not competitive with the local road network.

Rail services are under-developed, although some key services are provided for the port facilities. North-to-south connections are improving for large shipments and long haul. The main connection between two big cities, Athens in the south and Thessaloniki in the north, is presently under reconstruction and modernisation. This work will substantially improve long-haul connections with foreign markets.

Air

Greece is well served by international carriers. The strong position of the national carrier does affect the overall performance of this sector, as ground facilities are not affected by Olympic Airways.

To show the development of the air freight market the figures below show the tonnage of freight carried by Olympic Airways from 1984 to 1987.

Year	Tonnes carried 000s
1984	52.2
1985	60.9
1986	57.0
1987	62.3

Express services

The express sector is not well developed in Greece, mainly owing to the high cost of developing overnight and second-day services to this limited market. The major players are present and often link Greek operations with their Middle East operations. East-to-west communications are good. Progress is being made in the infrastructure.

The number of express shipments from Greece has seen growth only in recent years, as shown below.

Year	Number of shipments millions
1981	—
1983	0.1
1987	0.4

Combined transport

The Greek combined transport industry is strongly affected by the seaports. The major sea-going shipping companies own and operate overland combined services. Dedicated transport services are available from these providers for inland services as well as worldwide transport.

Summary

Greece is predominantly a seaman's transport market. The concentration of industry and commerce near the port cities has caused congestion and infrastructure problems. The recent trend is to decentralise. New industry is going to the fringes and outlying areas and, therefore, is dependent upon road transport.

On the international level, the importance of Greece as a transportation centre is increasing owing to its strategic position as a link between Western Europe and the Middle East.

Italy

The Italian market has long been characterised by the developed north and the undeveloped southern region. This split has been changing in recent years as the southern region has shown significant growth and improvement in transport infrastructure. The industrial and agricultural regions of the north have grown significantly in terms of output. However, infrastructure improvements have not kept pace with the growth in demand.

In 1985 the total quantity of goods transported by national transport organisations in Italy was over 1,050 million tonnes. Figure 27 shows the breakdown by transport mode.

Figure 27: Total quantity of goods transported by national transport organisations in Italy in 1985 by mode

Mode of transport	Million tonnes	Percentage
Rail	48.4	4.61
Road	1,000.0	5.24
Inland waterways	1.6	0.15
Total	1,050.0	100

Road

The major motorways of Italy are operated jointly by the state and the private sector. User fees in the form of tolls are used to finance investment in improvements and expansion of the present network. Because of its geographic position, Italy serves as an important link to Yugoslavia as well as the Mediterranean trading region.

Road transport is particularly important to the manufacturing sector in the northern region around Milan, Turin and Genoa. Over 50 per cent of all freight loaded in these regions is directed to France and West Germany.

Figure 28: Total traffic by group of goods and mode of transport in Italy

	Road	Rail	Inland waterways	Total
Cereals	n/a	1,652	–	1,652
Potatoes, fresh/frozen fruit, vegetables	n/a	1,379	–	1,379
Live animals, sugar beet	n/a	449	–	449
Wood, cork	n/a	3,056	–	3,056
Textiles, man-made fibres	n/a	274	–	274
Foodstuffs, animal fodder	n/a	2,006	–	2,006
Oil seeds, oleaginous fruits/fats	n/a	171	–	171
Solid mineral fuels	n/a	968	–	968
Crude petroleum	n/a	2	–	2
Petroleum products	n/a	1,256	–	1,256
Iron ore, iron and steel waste	n/a	5,849	–	5,849
Non-ferrous ores and waste	n/a	311	–	311
Metal products	n/a	9,356	–	9,356
Cement, lime, building material	n/a	386	–	386
Crude and manufactured minerals	n/a	3,642	–	3,642
Natural and chemical fertilisers	n/a	914	–	914
Coals, chemicals, tar	n/a	236	–	236
Other chemicals	n/a	1,818	–	1,818
Paper pulp, waste paper	n/a	749	–	749
Transport equipment, machinery	n/a	2,151	–	2,151
Manufactures of metal	n/a	273	–	273
Glass, glassware, ceramic products	n/a	225	–	225
Leather, textile, clothing	n/a	1,238	–	1,238
Miscellaneous articles	n/a	10,059	–	10,059
Total	–	48,420	–	48,420

Specialised services, especially in the transport of valuable stone, is a particular strength of the Italian transport companies. Southern agricultural producers depend upon the roadway links to transport 60 per cent of their production to the northern markets.

Rail

The Italian rail system is used primarily for the transport of raw materials to the factories. Limited services connect the Sicilian port of Syracuse for the delivery of bulk chemical and petroleum products to the industrial regions. Infrastructure improvements are now under way, including major investment in the information systems which support the management of the railway system.

Air

Air transport services are somewhat limited. Rome and Milan provide excellent international connections and good ground facilities. Smaller cities such as Pisa and Syracuse have local airports which provide connecting freight services to the larger centres. The Italian air transport industry has made recent moves to improve cargo services. Alitalia have developed an air freight service, and the leading air express companies have also made substantial investments in Italy.

To show the development of the air freight market, the figures below show the tonnage of freight carried by Alitalia from 1984 to 1987.

Year	Tonnes carried 000s
1984	118.3
1985	126.5
1986	139.8
1987	144.1

Express services

Italy is becoming a major centre for express service companies. Demand has increased recently and projections for increased service levels and competition are among the highest in Europe.

Combined transport

The local combined transport organisation, Cemat, showed the following development in units dispatched during the years 1983–6.

Year	Number of units
1983	9,607
1984	11,723
1985	11,989
1986	15,089

Percentage change 1985–6 = 25.8%

Summary

Italy represents a major market for international transport companies. The growth of the industrial base and the strategic geographic position of Italy is cause for new investment to bring infrastructure up to satisfactory levels. The distribution networks are increasing service quality to the south and from the north to international markets. Local freight is mainly carried by road.

Portugal

The breakdown of goods transported by rail, road and inland waterway is as follows:

Rail	40 per cent
Road	38 per cent
Inland waterways	22 per cent

Road

The main Portuguese motorways connect the industrial and agricultural production region of the north around Oporto to the capital, Lisbon. The growth of the Portuguese economy has put an extra strain on this busy route. Renewed interest in the coastal waterway and the rail network is likely to delay major improvements in the road system.

International connections to Spain are adequate, but the preference for other modes of transport has kept the total of goods shipped internationally by roadway to not more than 35,000 tonnes annually.

Rail

The Portuguese rail system is a strong one, developed mainly for the transport of passengers. The statistics for freight carriage are not available. However, industrialists and agriculture companies depend upon the state railway for long-haul connections. The main routes are north and south between Lisbon and Oporto and also between these two cities and major destinations in Spain.

The rail network has a good reputation for dependability and cost. Intermodal connections focus on the port facilities as opposed to motorway or airport connections.

Inland waterways

Portugal's agricultural community had a long tradition of transporting products to market and to distillery by boat. This mode of transport has diminished since the development of major motorways serving the industrial and agricultural regions, especially the northern districts. Increasing environmental awareness and increasing time delays due to congestion are expected to result in the re-opening of some water routes, especially in the port wine industry around Oporto.

Although inland waterways are not presently a dominant means of transport, it must be noted that Portugal's position as a seaport country makes it very attractive for manufacturers who wish to produce here and ship by coastal routes to northern markets. Port operators and the central government are promoting the advantages of this aspect of the transport network.

Air

Portugal's air connections are dominated by the state airline, TAP. With a limited international air network, TAP connects to other major carriers at key hubs in Europe. TAP has followed its industrial clients to establish links in more ports of call in Europe in order to profit from cargo deliveries.

Other European carriers fly daily and weekly non-stop services to all major airports, including Lisbon, the capital and centre of commerce, and Oporto, the northern industrial centre. Some tourist charter companies are now moving freight in and out of Portugal on tourist flights.

To show the development of the air freight market, the figures below show the tonnage of freight carried by TAP from 1984 to 1987.

Year	**Tonnes carried 000s**
1984	28.5
1985	30.0
1986	32.3
1987	35.1

Express services

The Portuguese express services industry is slow to develop. The relative high costs of operating courier services to and from the two main commercial centres is attributable to low volume potential and relative long distance to major express hubs. Strong rail and road connections between north and south Portugal appear to meet the need for internal express deliveries. The growth outlook is forecast to be low.

The Republic of Ireland

The Republic of Ireland has become one of the most profitable centres of investment in Europe, particularly in the manufacturing assembly sector. This is largely due to strong air and sea transport connections. The historical isolation of the country has been largely overcome by effective use of ports of entry as distribution centres.

International and internal transport services are well developed and efficient. Ireland has the highest level of road networks per capita within the EC. Public road and rail services are operated by subsidiaries of the national transport company, Coras Iompair Eireann (CIE), providing passenger and freight services between major towns and cities. There are cross-border links with Northern Ireland.

In 1985 the total quantity of goods transported by national transport organisations in the Republic of Ireland was 94.5 million tonnes. Figure 29 shows the breakdown by mode.

Figure 29: Total quantity of goods transported by national transport organisations in the Republic of Ireland in 1985 by mode

Mode of transport	Million tonnes	Percentage
Rail	3.4	3.59
Road	91.1	96.41
Inland waterways	—	—
Total	94.5	100

Road

The road system in Ireland is sufficiently developed to meet the needs of business and industry in Dublin and the other ports. Modern motorways serve only the route from Dublin to Naas, and around

Figure 30: Total traffic by group of goods and mode of transport in the Republic of Ireland

	Road	Rail	Inland waterways	Total
Cereals	1,915	–	–	1,915
Potatoes, fresh/frozen fruit, vegetables	1,297	–	–	1,297
Live animals, sugar beet	1,870	178	–	2,048
Wood, cork	1,876	–	–	1,876
Textiles, man-made fibres	520	5	–	525
Foodstuffs, animal fodder	19,451	230	–	19,681
Oil seeds, oleaginous fruits/fats	69	–	–	69
Solid mineral fuels	2,877	–	–	2,877
Crude petroleum	–	–	–	–
Petroleum products	4,943	80	–	5,023
Iron ore, iron and steel waste	216	36	–	252
Non-ferrous ores and waste	73	650	–	723
Metal products	613	18	–	631
Cement, lime, building material	16,441	580	–	17,021
Crude and manufactured minerals	22,733	251	–	22,984
Natural and chemical fertilisers	3,426	285	–	3,711
Coals, chemicals, tar	178	–	–	178
Other chemicals	857	201	–	1,058
Paper pulp, waste paper	119	–	–	119
Transport equipment, machinery	1,432	4	–	1,436
Manufactures of metal	358	–	–	358
Glass, glassware, ceramic products	180	–	–	180
Leather, textile, clothing	2,015	3	–	2,018
Miscellaneous articles	7,667	858	–	8,525
Total	91,126	3,379	–	94,505

Cork and Waterford, to serve the new industrial developments. However, with the assistance of the European Commission's Regional Industrial Development programme, new trunk roads are funded and under construction.

Rail

The main rail links are between Dublin and Cork, and there is a very important junction around Limerick serving the trading and population centres as well as the ports of Galway. The rail system carries mainly foodstuffs, animal fodder and peat.

Air

Rapid air services are available to all European and major world markets. The Republic of Ireland has four international airports, at Dublin, Shannon, Cork and Knock. In addition, there are a number of small airports and airfields capable of accepting executive and light aircraft.

Express services

The Republic of Ireland presently supports a low volume of express freight shipments. This is largely attributable to low population and the small size of commercial centres. Although the country is served by major courier companies, no major growth is forecast.

Combined transport

Seaports handle the greater part of Ireland's international trade. Dublin the major port, has been influenced by developing roll-on roll-off facilities which link with overland transport modes. Efficient intermodal networks include the air transport sector.

Summary

As an island, Ireland has inherent transport restrictions. However, effective infrastructure development has overcome many of the limitations. Air and ground links are good and efficient and the communications infrastructure provides Ireland with a very good transport network.

Spain

Spain's industry and agricultural producers have turned to road transport as the central government plans to build another 20,000 kilometres of trunk roads in the next ten years. The growth of the Spanish economy has been accelerated by its membership of the EC and the run-up to 1992.

The breakdown of goods transported by road and rail is as follows:

Rail	26.4 per cent
Road	73.6 per cent

Road

Road transport has shown strong growth in recent years: 1986 exhibited a 27 per cent increase in domestic transport on 1980 figures, from 99 million tonnes/kilometre to 126 million, while demand for transport by rail has been static.

The supply of road transport services is very fragmented. There are 161,000 road transport companies in Spain, of which 80 per cent have one vehicle. Only 420 companies have more than twenty vehicles. The larger companies all sub-contract part of their work to the numerous owner/drivers. Dangerous goods and special merchandise present demand for road tankers and dedicated transport vehicles.

Rail

Spain's railway system has been separated from the rest of Continental Europe's system owing to a nineteenth-century decision to protect Spain from northerly invasion by making the gauge of the railways different. Decisions have been taken by the transport minister to correct this and to rebuild the Spanish railways to meet the demands of the rising economy. For the present, there are additional costs involved in transferring goods to waiting train cars at the border. The logical choice for long-haul transport has been the coastal route. The attractiveness of the south of Spain for production facilities has had nothing to do with train connections and very much to do with coastal transport to northern markets.

Air

Spain is well served by European and international airlines. Labour disputes in recent years have led to delays and related costs in both passenger transport and cargo transport. Airport freight handling facilities are being improved, attention being given to intermodal connections to trunk roads. Bilateral agreements and the deregulation of the European airline systems are beginning to give cost breaks to the airlines serving this market. As some European airlines and express freight companies begin to develop their overland capabilities, the northern European markets will be much more accessible for Spanish producers.

Express services

The growth potential for express services in Spain is one of the highest in the world. The development of good processing facilities at airports and the influx of many international companies into Spain in recent years have attracted the major operators. The growth in demand for express services will be fuelled by new production facilities for components to be assembled at factories in the other European markets. Warehousing and transport time for components made in Spain will be cut to a minimum with modern express distribution methods. The annual growth rate of this segment in Spain will be over 40 per cent in the coming years.

Combined transport

Growth in combined transport mirrors economic growth and the development of major trunk roads stemming from seaport and airport facilities. Some of the leading road transport companies are beginning to offer more comprehensive services, including combined transport and warehousing facilities.

The local combined transport organisation, Transnova, showed the following development in units dispatched during the years 1983–6.

Year	Number of units
1983	8,610
1984	10,473
1985	9,592
1986	11,537

Percentage change 1985–6 = 20.2%

Summary

Spain will continue to be difficult for newcomers wishing to develop transport links. A very strong and increasing demand is facing a fragmented supply. The long-term future is bright, as the infrastructure is being designed to meet future demand.

Index